Living a Country Year

Living a Country Year

Wit and Wisdom
from the Good Old Days

Jerry Apps

WISCONSIN HISTORICAL SOCIETY PRESS

Published by the Wisconsin Historical Society Press
Publishers since 1855

The Wisconsin Historical Society helps people connect to the past
by collecting, preserving, and sharing stories. Founded in 1846,
the Society is one of the nation's finest historical institutions.
Join the Wisconsin Historical Society: wisconsinhistory.org/membership

First edition published 2007 by Voyageur Press
Wisconsin Historical Society Press edition 2018

For permission to reuse material from *Living a Country Year* (ISBN 978-
0-87020-861-4; e-book ISBN 978-0-87020-862-1), please access www
.copyright.com or contact the Copyright Clearance Center, Inc. (CCC),
222 Rosewood Drive, Danvers, MA 01923, 978-750-8400. CCC is a not-for-
profit organization that provides licenses and registration for a variety of users.

Printed in the United States of America
Cover: *For Jeremiah Williams* by Andy Fletcher. 2015. Oil on canvas. 42" x 60"
Cover design by Sara DeHaan
Typesetting by Shawn Biner

22 21 20 19 18   1 2 3 4 5
Library of Congress Cataloging-in-Publication Data
Names: Apps, Jerold W., 1934– author.
Title: Living a country year : wit and wisdom from the good old days / Jerry
  Apps.
Description: Wisconsin Historical Society Press edition 2018. | Madison :
  Wisconsin Historical Society, 2018.
Identifiers: LCCN 2017037406 (print) | LCCN 2017046743 (e-book)
  | ISBN 9780870208621 (E-book) | ISBN 9780870208614 (pbk. : alk.
  paper)
Subjects: LCSH: Country life—Anecdotes. | Farm life—Anecdotes.
Classification: LCC GT3470 (ebook) | LCC GT3470 .A67 2018 (print) |
  DDC 307.72—dc23
LC record available at https://lccn.loc.gov/2017037406

For Ruth

Contents

Acknowledgments

My brothers, twins Donald and Darrel, who appear in my stories many times, helped me to remember many of the details of the years when we were growing up on a small farm in central Wisconsin. We didn't always agree about what happened and when, but we agreed on the gist of the stories.

A special thank you to my wife, Ruth, a home economist, who tested all the recipes in this book. Occasionally, she had to make sense out of my mother's and grandmother's recipes, where the instructions included a pinch of this and a pinch of that and season to taste. Ruth also read the entire manuscript several times, pointing out errors and making suggestions for improvement. Additionally, I want to thank Opal Kunz, Carol Marting, and Ellen Schroeder, all home economists, who read and suggested improvements for the recipes, especially the directions.

My daughter, Susan, is a school reading specialist and a stickler for accuracy. I appreciate her careful reading of the manuscript. My son Steve is a journalist and staff photographer for the *Wisconsin State Journal*. He read for meaning and logic and straightened me out several times. Jeff, my younger son, served as an important sounding board for many of the ideas in this book.

Danielle J. Ibister, Voyageur Press/MEI editor, once more took my work and gave it her magic touch. I so much appreciate her efforts to make the book as readable as possible.

Introduction to the New Edition

In 2005 I published my book *Every Farm Tells a Story*, a collection of stories and memories inspired by my mother's meticulous farm account books. The book was so well-received by readers that my editors at Voyageur Press asked if I would be interested in writing a follow-up volume, telling more stories of my growing-up years on the farm in the 1930s through the early 1950s.

My wife, Ruth, and I came up with the idea of telling another round of stories based on the seasons of the year. Each season would include some of my mother's recipes from those days, along with bits of wisdom I had picked up from my father and other farmers I knew. We called the book *Living a Country Year: Wit and Wisdom from the Good Old Days*, and Voyageur Press published it in 2007. One reviewer wrote, "The meat of this new book is lovely stories about being a country boy, contemplation about the ways of nature and sage dollops of advice, sometimes delivered with gentle, dry humor. From [the author's] thoughts for May: 'Do nothing in haste, except running away from an angry dog.'"

Living a Country Year became the featured book in several "community read" projects. The Fond du Lac Public Library chose it for its community-wide read in 2009. As a capstone event, the library sponsored a chili supper using recipes from the book. After the supper, I spoke to more than two hundred people who had attended, sharing some of my stories, answering their questions, and enjoying many of their stories about life on the farm.

Of the many reader comments I received about this book, I have been most pleased when people tell me that it helped them remember their stories. As one reader wrote, "*Living a Country Year* reaffirms our rural heritage." I am delighted that the Wisconsin Historical Society Press is publishing this new edition.

Preface

Many of us, whether we live in a city or a small town, are searching for the simplicity that was once a part of country life. I grew up on a farm during a simpler time. The days were long, and the work was hard. We had no electricity, indoor plumbing, or central heating—conveniences we have long since taken for granted. Though it may have been a simpler time, it was certainly not an easier time. I'm often asked, "Weren't you miserable every day of the year, as you worked by the dim light of a kerosene lantern, hiked a mile along a country road to a one-room country school, walked for hours behind a team of work horses, and were lucky to get to town for a couple hours on a Saturday night?"

Some of that life was difficult, especially in the dead of winter when the temperature skidded to twenty below zero and the only warm place on the farm was in the barn with the cows and horses. Farm work could also be boring, especially to a kid: picking cucumbers, hoeing potatoes, husking corn by hand. Other work was exciting and fun: working on a threshing crew, driving a new tractor, and hauling grist to the mill for grinding.

Even with all the hard work, we had more time (perhaps *took* more time) to enjoy what was all around us: nights filled with starlight, days with clear blue skies and puffy clouds. Wonderful smells everywhere—fresh mown hay, wildflowers, and apple blossoms. Interesting sounds—the rumble of distant thunder, an owl calling in the woods, a flock of Canada geese winging over in the fall.

Our family was very close. We worked together, lived together, and played together. We depended on one another and cared for one another. We were also close to our neighbors, even though some lived several miles away. We helped them; they helped us.

Many of the thoughts in this book come from growing up and living in the country and knowing farmers and small-town people. As a kid I especially enjoyed the stories told around the wood-burning stove, shared during meals in threshing season, or merely swapped over the back fence. Other ideas come from my present farm near Wild Rose, located a few miles from where I grew up.

My father was a great storyteller as well as a country philosopher. He had only a sixth-grade education, yet he was full of words of wisdom and one-liners that had deeper meaning. Pa also had a deep appreciation for nature and the outdoors. He was keenly aware of the changing seasons and all the new smells, sounds, sights, and tastes.

I begin each month of *Living a Country Year* with a memory from my childhood days on a small central Wisconsin dairy farm during the years just before, during, and after World War II. After the stories, I include some personal outdoor experiences, country aphorisms, and even an occasional recipe.

A few years ago, I was signing copies of my book *Country Wisdom* at a bookstore. A young woman with two boys, probably eight and ten years old, stood in line. When she got to my table, she said, "Could I talk to you afterward?" I said, "Sure." This had happened to me before, and usually it meant the person had found an error or misspelling in my book or they disagreed with something I had written.

When I finished signing books, the woman and her boys came up to my table. She introduced them to me, and I shook their hands. I braced myself for what she had to say. "We live in the city," she began. "After we bought your book, every weekend we would travel to one of the nearby county parks. My husband, the boys, and I would read from your book. Then I would ask the boys what the words meant. We had a wonderful time helping our sons understand the ways of country living and the beliefs and values associated with it."

I was without words, an uncommon thing for a writer. I finally muttered, "Thank you."

My hope is that readers will find *Living a Country Year* another doorway to understanding life in the country—that they will find some enjoyment in these stories and gain some idea of country ways. And perhaps they will see their own busy lives from a new perspective.

January

Memories of Winter

For those of us who grew up in the north, January was usually a long, cold, and snowy month. The nights were dark and long, the days short and often cloudy. We farm kids had regular chores: cows to milk and feed, the barn to clean, eggs to gather, chickens to feed, wood boxes to fill, pigs to feed, and water to carry from the pump house to the house. With each new snowfall, we had paths to shovel from house to barn, barn to straw stack, barn to granary, granary to chicken house, chicken house to house, house to pump house, pump house to barn, and barn to hog house. A circle of shoveled paths connected the farm buildings and made chores a bit easier than they would be if we had had to wallow through sometimes waist-deep snow.

With the morning chores finished, we ate a huge breakfast— bowls of homemade oatmeal, followed by pancakes piled high on our plates and drenched in syrup. We ate strips of bacon that had been fried in a big, black cast-iron skillet that sat over the hottest part of the woodstove. We downed thick slices of homemade bread, sometimes toasted. The toaster was a foursided metal affair that stood over an open hole where a stove lid had been removed on the cookstove. Someone had to watch the toast because, depending on the fire, it could quickly brown and begin burning or sit quietly soaking up the wood smoke and scarcely turning color. Usually, though, we ate the thickly sliced pieces of homemade bread without toasting them; we smeared them with butter and homemade jam—strawberry, raspberry, or grape.

Then we changed from chore clothes to school clothes—heavy wool socks, six-buckle rubber boots, hand-knitted mittens and scarves, wool caps with earlaps, and warm mackinaw wool coats. No matter how cold or snowy it was, every day my brothers and I walked to the Chain O' Lake one-room country school. It was about a mile from our farm, and school was in session from nine to four. The school never closed for bad weather; there was no such thing as a snow day. But there were lots of snowy days, and sometimes, during blizzards, school let out early in the afternoon so the children could walk home while it was still daylight.

Back at home, the evening chores were mostly repeats of those we did in the morning. Day after day, week after week, each school day was the same.

One year toward the end of January, the temperature climbed above freezing for three or four days, and then it rained. The huge piles of snow that had accumulated since November shrank, and meltwater accumulated in the hollows on our farm, forming small lakes. Even the country road that trailed by our place got mushy for a few days, but the snow never completely disappeared. Then the temperature dropped back to zero, and the lakes in our fields froze solid.

Pa asked me and my brothers, with a twinkle in his eye, if we might want to spend some of our saved money on ice skates. "Those field ponds would make great skating rinks," he said.

The village of Wild Rose made a skating rink each year on one end of the sawmill property. My younger brothers and I had never skated before, but we had watched skaters spin around that rink.

Pa told us that as a kid he had skated and we might like to try it. He said he had checked at Hotz's Hardware in town. It had skates—the kind that clamped to the bottom of your shoes and were tightened in place with a little key that you carry in your pocket—for fifty cents a pair.

My brothers and I each spent fifty cents of our hard-earned savings and were soon trying out our skates on the big pond just down the hill from our house. Those first few attempts at skating bordered on disaster. I don't recall ever falling down as many times as I did that day, not even when ice fishing on slippery lakes. About the second or third day of our skating adventures, Pa asked if he could give it a try. I said, "Sure," looking forward to seeing the old man fall on his keister. As we stumbled, slipped, slid, and fell this way and that, Pa skated around the pond with nary a slip or a slide. He even turned around and skated backwards—a performance that truly amazed us. My brothers and I stood there with our mouths gaping. I asked Pa where he'd learned to skate like that. He didn't answer, just smiled.

Pa was full of surprises, his skill on skates being but one of them. I immediately looked forward to skating backwards, but first I decided I must learn to skate forward. My brothers and I practiced diligently until spring caused our pond to disappear. By that time, the three of us had become fair to middling skaters. My brother Darrel even graduated to figure skates and did all kinds of fancy maneuvers on the ice. I was content to move forward without falling and, after many hours of practice, even skate backwards.

The next winter, January marched along without so much as a day above freezing; indeed, there was a stretch of ten days or so when the thermometer didn't crawl above zero. So no ponds formed in the low places in our farm fields. That winter our skates hung on a nail in the woodshed.

Then one day, about mid-January, Jim Kolka, his brother Dave, and my brothers talked at school recess about how we missed ice skating and how we'd probably forgotten how to do it. Jim suggested that we skate on Chain O' Lake, which was located about a half mile south of the school and thus about a mile and a half from our farm. For the Kolka boys, who lived west of our place, the distance was more like two and half miles. We agreed on a night when we'd gather at Chain O' Lake and invite some of the other kids from school to come—Nita and Joyce Dudley, Mildred Swendrzynski, Clair Jenks. We'd shovel the snow off the lake and have an ice-skating party.

With the milking done and the cows fed and bedded down for the night, my brothers and I bundled up in our wool mackinaw coats, rubber boots, wool caps, and wool mittens that our grandmother Witt had knitted and given to us as Christmas presents. It must have been a Wednesday or a Thursday, and it was a night with a near full moon. In those days, before electricity came to our community, moonless nights were as dark as the inside of a barrel with both ends closed. When the moon was out, its cool bluish light reflected off the snow-covered fields; a clear, moonlit night in winter was almost as bright as day. The cold snow squeaked underfoot as we walked along the road piled high with snow on each side. It was like walking in a snow tunnel with the top open to the moonlight. Along with my skates, I carried a grain shovel from our granary.

When we arrived at the lake, someone had already started a fire, and the flames provided a yellow light to compete with the light of the moon. A plume of gray smoke drifted skyward. Clair Jenks was already shoveling snow to the side, exposing the smooth lake ice. I joined him with my shovel, as did Jim when he and his brother arrived. Soon we had a good-sized area exposed. I pulled off my six-buckle boots and clamped the ice skates to the bottom of my shoes, tightening them as much as I could, my cold hands fumbling with the little key.

Soon we were all on the ice, skating and laughing, falling down and getting up, and stopping by the fire to warm our hands before going onto the ice once more. Occasionally, a loud booming noise would start on one side of the lake and then cut all the way across.

Anyone not accustomed to the sounds of lake ice contracting in the cold would run to shore, but we had all heard lakes "talk" before. Sometimes a crack in the ice would appear as we watched, but we knew there was no danger as we continued skating.

We were all standing around the glimmering coals of the fire when we heard it. At first I thought it was another ice contraction. "What's that noise?" I asked Jim. "What noise?" he replied.

"That growl."

"I don't hear a growl," Jim said. "I heard it," Mildred said.

"I heard it, too," said Joyce Dudley.

I heard it again and this time knew it was definitely not caused by the lake ice. The sound came from deep in the woods surrounding the lake.

"I heard it again," I said.

"You're hearing things," Jim said, usually skeptical of unusual things I sometimes heard and saw.

"What could it be?" Joyce asked. She had concern in her voice.

"Likely nothing to worry about," Clair said. He was the oldest of our group.

Then we heard it once more, a deep growl, different from what a dog would make, a sound I had never heard before. And it was coming closer.

"What should we do?" Mildred asked.

"I say take off our skates and run like the dickens," Jim said. He obviously had heard the sound this time.

That's what we did. Before you could say "cold fingers don't work fast," we had our skates off, our boots on, and were headed through the woods, onto the country road, and home. My brothers and I probably ran the first half mile of the trip before we decided that nothing was trailing us in the dark.

"Well, how it'd go?" Pa asked when we got home. "Something was after us," my little brother Darrel said. We were all three out of breath.

"Chasing you?"

"Yup, growling and chasing us," I said. "Came out of the woods by the lake. Sounded like a bear or maybe a wolf." Of course I had never heard either a wolf or a bear growl so my reply was purely conjecture, but I thought it sounded plausible.

"Bear or wolf?" Pa said, a smile spreading across his face. He was sitting by the kitchen woodstove, his feet propped up on the open oven door.

"That's what I think it was," I said. "Sure sounded mean. We took off our skates and ran home when we heard it."

"Did you know that Miles Buelow's hired man lives in a shack near the lake? He cuts wood every day, has Sunday off when he walks back to Buelow's for a good meal and some clean clothes."

"No, I didn't know that," I said.

"Could be the hired man was having a little fun with you kids. Gets pretty lonely living in that little shack."

Later, Pa told Miles Buelow about what had happened at the lake, and the hired man had said how he had scared the bejeebers out of a bunch of kids who had been skating.

I never shared that information with Jim Kolka and the other kids. Sometimes it's fun to have some secrets. We skated several times more that winter on Chain O' Lake, but always in the daytime and on a Sunday. The hired man wasn't in his shack on Sundays.

January Thoughts

~ January is for slowing down and reflecting, for considering the year that has passed and anticipating the year that is beginning.

~ Start a journal and write in it every day, or at least once or twice a week. A journal is a place to record the weather, pen your thoughts, write a story from your past, copy some clever words from the newspaper, and write down a story you've heard.

~ Visit a county or state park, perhaps one your family visited last summer. Note how different it is with fewer people, dormant trees, and snow-covered trails.

~ Laughing out loud at least once a day, every day, all year long, is a first-rate New Year's resolution. You might enjoy it so much you'll want to continue into the following year and the year after that.

~ Reread a book you liked as a child: *The Adventures of Huckleberry Finn, Anne of Green Gables, Robinson Crusoe, The Swiss Family Robinson.* You will be amazed how the book has changed since you last read it.

~ Enjoy a bowl of homemade chili.

～ Take time to see the whiteness of fresh fallen snow that sparkles and glimmers and covers the grime and dirt of an earlier day. It's nature's way of hiding human dirt and clutter.

～ Whether climbing up a ladder or coming down, it is equally frightening.

～ North country saying: "When the days lengthen, the cold strengthens."

～ Slip on cross-country skis and explore a trackless trail, where the wind caresses the snow and the cold keeps you moving.

～ Watch the sun set when the temperature is below freezing. The sky is a steel blue that turns black as the sun sinks away and the thermometer plummets.

～ Listen for the silence of winter, when the snow buries the land and the cold tightens its grip, turning breath into clouds and thickening the ice on the lakes. There is great beauty in silence, something that we have little of these days.

～ When you walk in a woods after a fresh snowfall, you'll see a landscape of animal tracks—deer, cottontail rabbit, ruffed grouse, wild turkey. The tracks tell you about each animal's activities, showing where the animal has been and where it is headed, just as the tracks we leave in our lives speak of what we've done and where we've done it.

～ Stand in a snowstorm and watch snowflakes accumulate on your sleeve. Each snowflake is different, each one special—a reminder of nature's creative magnificence.

～ Everything has an end, except a sausage, which has two.

～ Sometimes doing nothing is the most important thing we can do.

- Try ice skating if for no other reason than to show that you still can move on thin steel runners.

- My father said about neighbors, "No matter how different your neighbor's lifestyle is from yours and how easy it is to criticize what they do and how they do it, they are still your neighbors. One day you may need their help, as they may need yours."

- Fear can be our worst enemy. Nothing cripples more than fear.

- Sit by a fireplace or woodstove doing nothing except listening to the occasional pop of the fire and smelling the hint of wood smoke that sneaks into the room.

- On a cold and snowy day, when the wind is whistling around the corners of my cabin, I crowd up to the woodstove with a copy of Henry David Thoreau's *Walden*. I read about his days in a rustic cabin on Walden Pond. I am with him as he writes about his bean patch, the pond in the winter, and the power of solitude. I read the words slowly, carefully, and sit back and reflect on their meaning. I think about the connection of words written in 1854 to today's world, to my life.

- Share a story from your youth. Paint a word picture of how it was when you were a kid, making no judgments about your childhood being good or bad, but merely showing what it was, unembellished and truthful—something for your personal historical record. Perhaps write your story in your journal.

- No matter how right I think I am about something, there is always someone who holds the exact opposite view, but thinks he or she is just as right. It's taken me a long time to realize that people can get along with each other even when they differ on so many things—but it often takes some doing, and some tongue biting.

↜ After a new snowfall, walk along the edge of a field, looking for little raised tunnels that twist through the snow. Field mice made these tunnels as they searched for food. The snow cover protected them from hawks that also searched for a meal.

MA'S HOMEMADE CHILI

1 pound ground beef
1 medium onion, chopped
1 cup macaroni
1 quart V-8 vegetable juice
1 (16-ounce) can kidney beans, drained and rinsed
1/2 teaspoon chili powder (could use more)
Salt and pepper to taste
1 tablespoon sugar

Brown ground beef and onion. Drain excess fat.

Cook macaroni in boiling, salted water about 8 minutes. Drain. Place V-8 juice in large kettle. Add beans, meat, onion, and cooked macaroni.

Stir in spices and sugar and simmer for 45 minutes. Add a little water if too thick.

Serves 4.

February

Grandpa Witt

Grandpa and Grandma Witt lived but a mile from our farm if you went straight across the fields, about a mile and a half if you followed the road. Their farm was even more hilly and stony than ours. The land included a gully large enough to bury several farm wagons and even a Model T Ford or two and leave nothing visible for those who drove up the long hill from County Highway A, along the dusty road to the Witt farm. Their farmstead was across the road from the Kolkas', which was an equally stony and hilly farm. (Earlier, they had farmed near Wisconsin Rapids, where the land was flat as a ballroom floor with nary a stone in sight. A question never answered was why they came to this rough and hilly farm some thirty miles to the east of their first farm.)

On these 120 acres, they raised three boys and three girls, one of them my mother. (One child died as a youngster.) Grandpa Witt was a tall, thin man with a head of white hair and a big white mustache. Grandma Witt was short and plump and always had her white hair tied in a bun behind her head. Grandpa's first name was William; everyone called him Bill. My grandmother's first name was Amelia. Although both Grandma and Grandpa were 100 percent German, they both were born in this country.

Grandpa Witt was a good farmer; people today would call him a progressive farmer because he was always trying new things. For instance, in the late 1930s, when the University of Wisconsin's county agricultural agent for Waushara County began promoting alfalfa as a hay crop for central Wisconsin, Grandpa Witt was one of the first to grow it. It was not an easy crop to grow in central Wisconsin, because alfalfa, unlike the common hay crops such as timothy and clover, required more alkaline soil—"sweeter soil," as some farmers described it. The sand lands of central Wisconsin were naturally acidic (sour), and alfalfa would not grow well until the land was made sweeter. To do that, farmers needed to apply lime or marl, which are forms of calcium carbonate.

Lime had to be hauled from the quarries of southeastern Wisconsin, and although the raw material was relatively inexpensive, by the time it got to central Wisconsin, transportation costs made it expensive. Chain O' Lake, about a half-mile south of the country school by the same name, had a marl bottom. Marl forms over thousands of years as snails and other shelled water creatures die and accumulate on the floor of some lakes. While many people knew marl was there, and some, such as the county extension agent, knew of its lime-like qualities, it was a problem to extract it from the bottom of the lake, which was twenty feet deep and deeper in places.

Grandpa Witt convinced several of his neighbors, including Pa, to hire a dredger to dig marl from the lake and pile it on shore. The machine, after many days of work, accumulated a huge pile of soggy marl, fondly known for years as "the marl pile," on the north shore of the lake. The neighbor-partners in the venture then divided the pile into as many sections as there were partners. With teams and steel-wheeled wagons, the farmers hauled the marl to the fields where they wanted to grow alfalfa. It was all hand work. Pitch the marl onto the wagon with a big scoop; pitch it off again in the field.

All the effort paid off. Grandpa Witt and his marl-partner neighbors were growing thick and lush alfalfa, yielding many times more hay than timothy and clover did, and providing a protein-rich feed for their milk cows. Grandpa's progressive idea paid off. Within a few years, all the farmers in the neighborhood were growing alfalfa.

These farmers hauled marl for several years, until lime became more readily available. Handling lime also required far less work. It came either in bulk—a truck dumped a load in your field and you shoveled it into a horse-pulled lime/fertilizer spreader—or you bought the lime in sacks and dumped them directly into the spreader. The marl pile at the lake was eventually abandoned, serving as a reminder to those who visited Chain O' Lake of Bill Witt's vision for better farming.

As a youngster, I always had fun walking with my mother to Grandpa's farm. Grandma always had molasses cookies for me. She also knitted me mittens, caps, and other woolen things. In her spare time, her knitting needles never stopped.

Visiting Grandpa's place was special for other reasons. With two exceptions, no one in our community had electricity until after World War II. Andrew Nelson had a wind charger, a windmill that powered an electrical generator, and Grandpa Witt had a Delco generator system powered by a gasoline engine. The generator charged a bank of glass batteries stacked on one end of Grandpa's pump house. It was a 32-volt system, compared to the 110-volt systems that we commonly know today.

With the Delco 32-volt system, not only did Grandpa have electric light bulbs in the house and barn and other outbuildings, but Grandma also had an electric iron and a washing machine powered with an electric motor. I marveled at these devices, because we lit our house with kerosene lamps and the barn with kerosene lanterns. I'm sure my mother marveled as well, because our washing machine was powered with a temperamental Briggs & Stratton gasoline engine that started when it wanted to, not when anyone else wanted it to. Ironing meant keeping the cookstove burning hot, even during the warmest days of summer, because the stove heated the sadirons for ironing. "Sadiron" is an appropriate name for those heavy hunks of metal (the dictionary says "sad" refers to heavy and compact). My mother had several of them. While she used one, three or more were heating on the stove. A removable handle allowed her to replace the one that had cooled with a fresh, hot one. It was stifling, hot, miserable work—sad by almost any definition.

One day, I heard mumblings that Grandpa wasn't feeling well and his heart was giving him problems. He died February 11, 1941, several months before the outbreak of World War II on December 7. Although the local furniture store, which also doubled as a funeral parlor, took care of the technical details, his casket stood in our living room until the day of the funeral. This was the first time I had ever seen a dead person. When I went to bed, I had to walk by the room where Grandpa lay in a satin-lined casket, flowers standing all around him. The sickly smell of flowers filled the living room and seeped out into the dining room and even up the stairway to my bedroom. I hurried by the parlor, trying not to peek in, but I always looked. The scene was always the same. Grandpa lay with his hands folded across his chest, his eyes closed like he was sleeping.

Neighbors and relatives stopped by constantly—in the morning, in the afternoon, and in the evening—because it seemed that everyone knew Bill Witt and wanted to pay their respects. Many of them brought along hot dishes, pies, cakes, cookies, and Jell-O salads so my mother didn't have to do any cooking during the time leading up to the funeral. My mother and father greeted them all and offered them something to eat. About the only farm work we did during those heartbreaking days was to milk the cows, do the barn chores such as feeding hay and silage and hauling manure, take care of the chickens, and feed the pigs. The rest of the time, we dealt with visitors who came by the house.

The funeral was February 15 at West Holden Lutheran Church, a country church located near Bean's Lake and about halfway between Wild Rose and Wautoma. The church was filled on that cold, blustery day. When the services were over, we moved to the gravesite, a spot under some big white pine trees on the north side of the cemetery. I held my mother's hand while the casket was lowered into the grave. My father held my twin brothers, who were just three years old at the time.

Now, many years later, I take my grandchildren to Grandpa and Grandma Witt's gravesite. (She died in December 1941.) The big white pines still stand, as they did then. And the memories flow as I talk about Grandpa and Grandma Witt and my memories of them.

February Thoughts

∽ For me, February is a time to remember my grandfather and famous presidents, honor my valentine, and celebrate a few days when the temperature may climb above freezing and the snow will turn soft.

∽ Try reading a book by candlelight, as Abraham Lincoln did when he was a child. It helps me remember that greatness has little to do with convenience.

∽ Don't believe two-thirds of what you hear, and say nothing about the rest.

∽ It's not the color of barn wood that makes a difference, but the strength of the wood that built it. Same with people.

∽ It's an old but important truism—to get along with others, avoid discussing religion, politics, and the strange relatives in their families. Your hope is that the person with whom you are talking has a similar philosophy, especially when it comes to your extended family.

∽ Sometimes it's important to just breathe deeply.

∽ It's interesting to record the time for the sunrise and sunset each day in February and note how the hours of daylight increase as winter moves ever so slowly toward spring.

～ If bigger is better, why is a dime worth more than a nickel?

～ Visit a frozen pond on a windy winter day. Watch the wind play with the snow on the ice, swirling it, lifting it, dropping it, making unending patterns. An unseen artist is at work—creating, forming, doing, undoing—never satisfied with the results.

～ It's not the shape of a bowl that makes it useful, but the space in it.

～ Some things to reflect on when the day is cold, snow is piled against the side of the house, and a northwest wind rattles the windows:

When the singer is gone, where do we go for the music?

Knowing when to stop doing something is often more difficult than knowing when to start.

Going slow is usually the way to go.

No one can steal a memory.

Wherever you go, that's where you are.

During a journey, often we discover another destination far more important than the one planned.

Sometimes the hardest thing to do is to keep doing.

It's easy to smile on a sunny day; it's the cloudy days that challenge us.

Look away from the bright lights; it is in the shadows that we find the timid and the thoughtful.

Listen for quiet comments; they offer a differing opinion and a powerful minority perspective.

Waiting for opportunity to knock on your door is like waiting for a train after the tracks have been torn up and the depot closed.

- Don't make too small a hole in the ice when ice fishing. Nothing is more embarrassing or perplexing than to hook a fish too large for the hole. Same with life. Be prepared for the big opportunities; they often come along when you least expect them.

- I've long enjoyed ice fishing, although I don't do it very often these days. Ice fishing is an excellent test of one's patience and an opportunity for unencumbered thinking, because fish usually bite slowly in winter.

- It's fun to recall your favorite toy when you were a child and why it was special. Write down your memory. It will bring back pleasant thoughts.

- I enjoy hiking in my woodlot on a crisp, sunny, snowy morning. Dead leaves, brown and tattered, hold fast to the oak trees. These limp and ragged oak leaves are nature's reminders of the previous season.

- Listen to the views of others, but trust your own as well.

- February is a good time to visit a homebound friend and share memories and stories. It'll be a cheering-up time both for your friend and for you.

- When the temperature hangs just above zero, listen for the sound of a chickadee calling its name over and over. A chickadee is a tough, persistent little bird with a black cap and a winter personality.

- I recall the afternoons I spent as a child sitting by the woodstove in the back of the hardware store in Wild Rose with my father, listening to the oldtimers spin stories of earlier days. It was a sharing of history that was personal and special, albeit embellished here and there with each telling. Around that old woodstove, I learned to appreciate the power and the joy of a good story.

～ Winter is the best time to split wood with a maul because the frozen blocks of wood split much easier than in summer. A special gift received from splitting wood is the smell—an aroma as distinctive as newly mown hay in summer, subtle yet powerful, earthy and real.

～ Strap on a pair of snowshoes and head up a quiet trail, one step at a time, each one measured and difficult but easier than walking in near waist-deep snow. I walk like a duck when snowshoeing, my feet farther apart than normal so the snowshoes don't clank together. I stop often and look back at my tracks, for as difficult as snowshoeing may be in fresh, deep snow, the tracks are something to behold. They look like the tracks of some prehistoric animal that has visited the land once again and chose winter to do it.

～ On a cold afternoon, page through a new seed catalog that has just arrived in the mail. It's an early reminder of summer, and its colorful pictures evoke both memories and promises.

～ Sometimes, when I am alone at my cabin, I dump a jar of sauerkraut into a cast-iron frying pan rubbed with bacon grease. I move it to the warmer part of the woodstove and soon am treated to the pungent smell of kraut frying, bubbling, and turning brown on the bottom. It's a reminder of my childhood, when my mother fried kraut. And we all ate it, too.

GRANDMA'S MOLASSES COOKIES

2 cups sugar
1 cup shortening
3 eggs
1 cup molasses
2 teaspoons cinnamon
1/2 teaspoon cloves
1/2 teaspoon ginger
1/2 teaspoon salt
2 teaspoons soda
4 to 4 1/4 cups flour

Blend sugar and shortening until fluffy.

Add eggs and molasses. Mix well.

Mix dry ingredients together.

Add flour mixture gradually to egg mixture (makes a stiff dough).

Refrigerate two hours or overnight.

Roll out part of the dough 1/4 inch thick on a floured pastry cloth. Keep the rest cold.

Cut with favorite cookie cutters. Place on a lightly greased cookie sheet. Brush each cookie top with beaten whole egg.

Bake 350 degrees for about 10 minutes.

March

The Old Mill

The old red mill in Wild Rose, Wisconsin, stands next to the dam that holds back Pine River and forms the millpond. Water tumbles over the spillway and twists through eastern Waushara County on its way to Lake Winnebago. The mill was built in 1873, the same year the village of Wild Rose was organized. Farmers in this part of the Midwest grew wheat, and this mill, like many water-powered mills, ground the tan kernels into flour. By the late 1870s, farmers discovered that they could no longer grow wheat profitably. This old mill and hundreds like it in the upper Midwest shifted from producing flour to grinding grist (ground grain) for dairy cattle.

Farmers gathered at the old mill once or twice a week to have their grist ground. The mill was a place for swapping stories, starting gossip, and discussing the ups and downs of farming. I accompanied my father to the mill many times, often on a Saturday when I was home from school. When the morning chores were done, we'd gather up an armful of gunny bags—burlap sacks, to be more formal—and head for the corncrib. I'd hold the sack open while Pa used a big scoop fork to shovel in the yellow cobs. I had to hold the sack just right to keep it open and keep the corn from spilling on the floor. We'd fill sack after sack, tying each one with a shank of binder twine. We'd use a miller's knot on the twine so that it would come untied with a quick tug.

When we had scooped full a half dozen sacks with corn, we'd move to the granary, where we filled several grain bags with oats. The cotton grain bags were longer than gunny sacks and more closely knit than the coarse burlap. Once more I'd hold the sacks open while Pa scooped the grain from the oat bins with a grain shovel.

Pa would start the old four-door 1936 Plymouth and drive it to the granary. He'd pull out the backseat and lean it against a grain bin. Then we'd stuff the sacks of oats and corn into the back of the car, and we'd be off to town—the back tires of the Plymouth halfway flat from the load. The snow would be melting, for it was March, and the country road would be muddy in the low places. Pa would gun the engine, and we'd slide through the mud; with all the weight in the car, the back wheels seldom slipped.

At the mill, we'd take our turn to unload our sacks of corn and oats. While we waited, we'd talk with the farmers already in line. Several of our neighbors would be there—Bill Miller, Andrew Nelson, Arlin Handrich—as well as farmers from the other side of town, people who Pa knew, but I didn't.

For me, the mill was a mysterious, exciting place. Water powered its mechanical parts, the inside of the building was filled with pulleys and belts, and the entire structure shook a little as the grinding mechanism operated. The maple wood floor was smooth from the hundreds of sacks of grain pulled across it over the years.

When our turn came, Pa would lift the sacks out of the back of the Plymouth and hoist them, one after the other, onto the mill platform. The miller, who in those days was Rodney Murty, would help dump the sacks into little square holes located on the mill floor. The grain rattled down a metal tube to the grinding wheels. An enclosed wooden chute about four inches square ran from the basement to the second floor of the mill; when the grinding was completed, the grist made its way to the top of the building by means of little cups fastened to a belt running inside this chute.

After a few minutes, we'd hang our sacks on the end of a little chute, and the sacks would be filled with the warm, sweet-smelling grist. When a sack was filled, we'd tie it shut and drag it across the floor to where it was weighed. (The miller was paid according to the pounds of grist ground.) After the weighing, we'd lift and shove the sacks back into the Plymouth. The entire grinding process took a little more than half an hour.

Having the grain ground was not the only reason for going to the mill. The stories and the visiting also attracted farmers to the mill, but none would say that was the reason. To a person, these farmers were storytellers, surpassed in ability only by the miller himself.

Rodney Murty often told the story of when the previous miller, Ed Hoaglin, brought electricity to Wild Rose. Hoaglin had built a little brick building alongside the mill and installed a water-powered electric generator in 1908. When the generator was installed, the homes and businesses in the village of Wild Rose had electricity. That one convenience—a few electric bulbs—created a tremendous gulf between the village and country people.

When the mill started generating electricity, Murty was Hoaglin's assistant. Murty helped string electric wires throughout the village, and nearly everyone replaced their kerosene lamps with electric bulbs. Villagers soon moved beyond electric bulbs to washing machines with electric motors and even electric irons. Because the mill was busy grinding grain all through the day, the electric generator was not turned on until after five o'clock in the afternoon, when the grinding shut down. Promptly at eleven each evening, the miller blinked the lights three times, pulled the switch, and shut off the generator. He said he had to build up a head of water in the millpond for the next day's grinding. Thus the electricity was on for only about six hours each day. Village women hurriedly washed clothes and ironed during the evenings.

As Murty told the story, a group of women marched to the mill one day at noon and asked to speak to Mr. Hoaglin. He went outside to talk with them, having no idea why a group of village women were visiting the mill, which was clearly a man's domain.

"We want the electricity on at noon," the leader of the women said.

"Whatever for?" Hoaglin asked. "It's broad daylight at noon."

"It's not for the light."

"For what then?"

"We want to iron clothes."

"Iron clothes?" the incredulous miller asked.

"Yes, iron clothes. We know you shut down milling during the noon lunch hour and we thought you could turn on the electricity then."

After considerable discussion, the women of the village got their way. It's difficult to turn down a group of women when they are united in what they want and determined not to return to their homes until they get the decision they want. One could imagine all the women in Wild Rose frantically ironing from twelve until one, when the electricity would be turned off until five o'clock that afternoon.

March was always a challenging month for the miller. In March, the snow melts, and the rivers, including the Pine River, often flow over their banks and send much more water into the millpond than is normal. The dam is at risk during these times, especially if the snowpack has been deep and the temperatures rise quickly for a few days.

Rodney Murty told this story that he had heard from Ed Hoaglin. It was in early March, after a long snowy winter. All week, the temperature climbed into the fifties each day; the snow quickly melted, and the millpond's water level rose steadily. The dam had been constructed of wood, soil, gravel, and rocks—

a structure vulnerable to high water. (Concrete hadn't yet become readily available for dams and other construction.) Five years before, the dam had washed out, and Hoaglin remembered it well. He almost lost the mill that time.

During this particular week of warm temperatures and melting snow, the threat to his mill was again real. The waters of Pine River began spilling over their banks by Wednesday. By Friday, many of the low areas along the river were already flooded.

Friday morning, Hoaglin watched a bank of clouds build in the west. Rain was coming. He was at the mill when the rain began falling—a heavy, steady rain. He would be there all that night.

Soon the millpond was spilling over its banks, flooding the land around it, and threatening to flood the homes built in the low areas nearby. As darkness fell, the rain continued, sometimes coming down so hard that Hoaglin couldn't see across the millpond. The millpond water kept rising.

After supper, John Protheroe, the village marshal, stopped by the mill. He also remembered well the last time the dam went out, nearly washing away the mill and flooding homes half a mile downriver.

"How's the dam doin'?" the marshal asked.

"Holdin' so far," Hoaglin said. "But if this rain keeps on, well, I don't know if she'll hold."

All night long, the miller and the marshal watched the rain and kept an eye on the millpond as the water kept rising. Every half hour or so, they headed outside to check the dam. In the gray hour before dawn on Saturday, the two men, with kerosene lanterns, walked along the dam.

"Trouble," yelled the marshal over the storm. Hoaglin hurried to where Protheroe was pointing. A trickle of water ran over the wet soil near the dam, beginning to tear a hole in the structure. With their shovels, the two men worked frantically to repair the damage, but with every hole patched, two or three more appeared.

"I think she's a goner," yelled the miller, wiping mud from his face.

"I'll go warn the people downstream," the marshal said as he hurried away.

Hoaglin returned to his mill, hoping that the rush of water would spare the building. In a few minutes, a huge breach in the dam appeared on the side farthest from the mill. Angry water gushed in a white, frothy torrent. The miller stood near the mill, rainwater dripping off his old felt hat, helpless to do anything but watch and hope.

In less than a half hour, the dam was gone, though the mill had been spared.

Over the years, Hoaglin had told the story many times. Though the mill dam was now made of concrete and steel and able to withstand spring snowmelt more effectively, once again Rodney Murty was reminded of what had happened.

Today the mill stands quietly on the banks of the Wild Rose millpond. Water tumbles over the dam's spilllway, and the little electric generator building is still there. The memories return as I stand and watch and listen to the soothing sound of the water make its way to Lake Winnebago and on to Green Bay and Lake Michigan.

March Thoughts

～ Take a casserole to an ailing neighbor. She will enjoy the food, and you'll both have a good time visiting.

～ In early March, listen for the first flocks of Canada geese winging north over the cabin in ever-changing Vs. They honk their happiness for the change of seasons and cooperate with each other as they fly, confident that they have judged correctly that they will not face one more snowstorm or blast of frigid air from the north. But they may be wrong.

～ Build a birdhouse. Have a child or a grandchild help you. Read about birdhouses and decide what kind to make. For a wren? A bluebird? Perhaps a tree swallow? Learn why different kinds of birds prefer different kinds of houses.

～ As the winter snow disappears, look for Princess Pine, a low-growing, shade-loving evergreen fern-like plant that thumbs its nose at winter and offers an island of green in a sea of brown leaves and dead grass.

～ When you begin too much, you accomplish little.

ᦔ There is a time to hurry and a time to slow down,
   A time to rest and a time for action,
   A time for thinking and a time for doing,
   A time to hear and a time to be heard,
   A time to speak and a time to listen.

ᦔ I met a fellow the other day who talked nonstop and didn't
   say a thing.

ᦔ March is a good month to create something new—a poem,
   a story, a wood carving, a quilt, a painting, a photograph, a
   piece of music—and feel better about yourself.

ᦔ It's okay to not know and admit it. Not knowing is the beginning of great wisdom.

ᦔ I smile when someone says it's been a wonderful winter because of the deep snow that provides spring moisture and
   the cold weather that kills off noxious bugs. I smile more
   when a few minutes later another person curses the deep
   snow and cold temperatures and can't wait until it's spring.
   Winter lovers, winter haters—all surviving together in the
   north, giving each other something to talk about.

ᦔ In March, listen for the first sandhill cranes on an above-
   freezing late afternoon as they return from their winter home
   in the southern states. These great cranes remind me of when
   dinosaurs roamed the earth and huge birds, relatives of the
   sandhills, flew over the land. I listen to their call—a chilling,
   exhilarating, nothing-else-like-it call that echoes in the valley and fills the air with the sounds of prehistoric times. It's
   a reminder that spring is near, although the snow-covered
   fields suggest otherwise.

ᦔ On a clear day, when the sun is warm and the snow is mushy,
   I walk with my grandson, and we listen for the sound of

melting snow water hurrying over stones that someone tossed in a gully to stop further washing. It's a warbling, gurgling, soothing sound. The water rushes with ever-greater intensity as the day progresses, until by mid-afternoon the sound reaches a crescendo—one more announcement that spring has arrived in the north.

~ Be leery of a string of warm days in March when the temperature soars into the fifties and the sky is as blue as summer. It is one of nature's tricks. Just when I think spring is finally here, winter comes roaring back, and I go looking for the snow shovel once more.

~ With the snow melted, thick frost covers everything on a chilly morning—the needles of the red pines, the bare branches of the white oaks, the brown stems of last year's grass smashed flat by the winter snows. In the background of this artistic place is a chorus of morning birdsong. And permeating it all is the fresh, promising smell of spring.

~ I visit my pond on a day when the wind is howling through the tops of the bare oaks and maples and tearing at the ice that is still present, weakening it, making it rubbery and unsafe, tearing hunks loose and pushing them to shore—releasing the grip of winter.

~ I smell spring after a day of drippy rain. The rainwater seeps into the ground, driving out the frost and sending forth the aroma of promise for the new season, a combination of smells from wet soil, dead leaves, and warm, fresh air. It's an almost-forgotten smell that enters the very core of one's being after a long winter.

~ On a day when snowflakes fly on a cold northwest wind and the robins are all fluffed up and not singing their usual daybreak song, still give spring credit for trying. The buds on the lilacs are near bursting, the daffodils are almost ready to pop, and the tiny red flowers on the maple tree are open and happy.

～ A pair of cottontail rabbits races around the yard, past the bird feeder, around the maple tree, into the lilac bushes. Fun to watch. Playing tag? Nope. My wife puts it straight: "Wait until all the little bunnies eat your garden, you'll have a different opinion." I know she is right.

～ Each day, I look for the first shoots of green on the south side of the cabin, where tulips are looking for spring even though there's a pile of snow only a few feet away.

～ I marvel at what an all-night rain in late March can do. It washes away the last remnants of old snow, wakes up the dormant grass in front of the cabin, sends spring flowers leaping out of the ground, and causes my spirits to soar.

～ After the snow has melted and before new growth has begun, my wife, Ruth, and I inspect the prairie I'm restoring. We see the bare stems of blazing star, the open pods of milkweeds—a few straggling seeds remaining—dried asters, brown goldenrod stems, and dead grass. I wonder how this land looked to the first settlers who plowed the soil with breaking plows and oxen and turned under the wild grasses and wildflowers that I am now encouraging to return.

～ On a warm day in late March, when there is little to do outside, Ruth and I sometimes visit the community cemetery and walk among the tombstones. It is a hillside of history and a studded pasture of stories. I note the names, many of people I once knew. One day my tombstone will be here, near my parents and grandparents, uncles and aunts, cousins and neighbors.

~ Learn how to leave some things alone.

~ If "everyone is doing it," then this might be the time to question whether you should.

~ Happiness comes from doing interesting and worthwhile things. Most of us find happiness when we are not looking for it.

KIDNEY BEAN AND HAMBURGER CASSEROLE

1 pound ground beef
1 onion, chopped
4 medium potatoes, peeled and sliced
1 (16-ounce) can kidney beans, drained and rinsed
1 (10 1/2-ounce) can condensed tomato soup
1/3 cup water

Butter a 2-quart casserole dish.
Brown ground beef. Drain excess fat.
Place beef in bottom of casserole.
Layer the onions, potatoes, and beans on top of the beef.
Mix soup with water until blended. Pour over top of vegetable layers. Cover.
Bake 350 degrees 45 to 50 minutes.
Serves 4 to 6.

April

Henry and His Model T

A little cloud of dust rolled up behind the strange-looking car that slowly made its way down our country road that warm, late-April day. The year was 1944, we were in the midst of World War II, and traffic was scarce during those months of gas and tire rationing. We usually saw the mailman and the milkman, and sometimes a neighbor drive by. And that was all.

As the car got closer, my brothers and I saw that it had no top—just a windshield to protect the driver from the elements. We could hear it chug, chugging along. The driver, a young-looking man, waved to us and turned into our farmyard.

"Hi, boys," the young man said. "This the Apps place?"

"It is," I answered. My younger brothers and I crowded up to this odd-looking, black, dusty car with no roof. The wheels had wooden spokes, and the tires were not much wider than a bicycle's. It stood high off the ground.

"What kind of car is this?" I asked.

"It's a Model T," the young man answered proudly. "A Model T Ford Touring Car. Best car on the road, bar none."

"Never saw a Model T before," I said. At the time, Pa drove a 1936 Plymouth.

"Probably because they don't make 'em anymore. Old Henry Ford has gone on to other kinds of cars. Made his last Model T in 1927. Your pa around?"

"He's down in the barn," I said. My brother Donald pointed to the barn.

I looked in the backseat of the car and saw a badly scuffed leather suitcase and a guitar.

"What's your name?" I asked.

"It's Henry—Henry Lackelt. You can call me Hank if you want."

Henry Lackelt was tall and thin and had an easy smile that lit up his face when he talked.

"You our new hired man?" I asked.

"I am, if your old man'll have me."

In the midst of the war, it was near impossible to find a hired man. Somehow, Pa had heard about Henry Lackelt and had written to him, asking him to come to the farm. In those days, a hired man worked from spring until fall, and then was on his way to find winter work in the cities or in the logging camps in the north, wherever work was available. We never found out why Henry hadn't been drafted for the war when almost all young men eighteen and older had been called up.

Pa hired him on the spot. Soon Henry was a part of the family, sitting at our table to eat meals and sleeping in the spare bedroom upstairs. Henry was a hard worker, and he knew how to handle horses, too, which was what we used to do our farm work during the war. But it was in the evening, when the cows were milked and turned out to pasture, and the cans of fresh milk were placed in the cooling tank, and the day's work was done, that we all especially enjoyed having Henry around.

We would gather on the back porch—Pa, Ma, my twin brothers and me, and Henry with his old, scratched-up guitar. He sat on the edge of the porch, crossed his legs, and strummed one string, then another, while he screwed on the little knobs at the top end of the instrument. Soon he announced, "Good enough." Then he ran a thumb across the strings and began playing and singing. He started with "That Silver-Haired Daddy of Mine," a beautiful old tune that I knew from the WLS Barn Dance that we listened to every Saturday night on our batterypowered Philco radio. "In a vine-covered shack in the mountains, bravely fighting the battles of time ..." The sound of the guitar and Henry's voice hung on the cool night air like the call of the whippoorwill that we often heard on summer evenings. His voice was among the best I'd ever heard, although I must admit that outside of the Barn Dance music and a country-western singer or two at the Waushara County Fair, I hadn't heard many guitar-strumming singers.

When the song was over, we all clapped. Then we sat quietly for a few minutes, feeling the cool night air moving up from the hollows and watching the mist rise over the alfalfa field in front of the house.

"Red River Valley" was next. "Come and sit by my side if you love me. Do not hasten to bid me adieu." It was such a beautiful tune, especially the way that Henry sang it.

Henry's Model T sat under the big elm tree just south of the house. The top was up to keep out the weather, and Henry had cleaned the trademark dull black paint to an attractive luster.

One Sunday afternoon a few weeks later, Henry was puttering with his Model T. It seemed something always needed adjusting.

"How do you drive this thing?" I asked.

"Nothing to it," Henry said. "Wanna give it a try?"

I was ten years old and here Henry was asking if I wanted to drive his prize Model T Ford car.

"Sure," I said, trying to sound much more confident than I felt. "How do you do it?"

"Step in and I'll show you."

I opened the door on the right and crawled onto the seat and peered out the windshield. Meanwhile, Henry was turning the crank that stuck out underneath the radiator on the front of the machine. The car coughed, sputtered, then caught. Henry raced around and adjusted the levers on either side of the steering wheel, then crawled in beside me. The engine chugged along quietly, as a typical four-cylinder engine will do.

"See these pedals on the floor?"

"Yup."

"See this big lever?" Henry touched a lever that was to the left of his seat.

"Yup."

"Well, that's it. Along with these two levers on the steering wheel, that's all you need to know. By the way, don't worry about the lever on the left of the steering wheel once you got her going. That's the spark. This lever on the right, that feeds the gas."

"Yup," I said again, becoming a bit confused with what the pedals and levers were all about.

"Watch what I do." Henry eased off the big parking brake lever on his left. Then he pushed his foot down on the leftmost floor pedal and pulled on the lever that fed the gas. The engine immediately sped up—*chug, chug, chug.* The car began moving. We headed past the barn and out to the big hayfield we had just harvested.

I was wondering when he would let me drive and what it would be like. But I didn't say anything.

"If you want to slow down, push the pedal to the right. That's the brake. And if you want to go in reverse, you push this middle pedal."

We drove a few hundred yards, when Henry stopped. "Your turn," he said.

We switched places, and he once more explained what I needed to do. Soon I was chugging across the hayfield, holding onto the steering wheel with both hands and keeping my foot pushed down on the leftmost pedal.

"Look out for stones," Henry said as we bounced along.

Nothing beat the fun I had that afternoon, driving around our alfalfa field with his Model T Ford, having my first experience driving a car.

The Model T had other features that made it especially attractive. On hot summer evenings after the work was done, Henry, my brothers, and I would pile into the Model T and drive the mile and half to Chain O' Lake, where we all went swimming. The car was a challenge to drive on sandy roads, because the front wheels would sometimes jackknife and give us all a thrill we hadn't looked forward to as Henry fought with the steering wheel to straighten it out. Fortunately, we probably never drove faster than twenty miles an hour, so we were in little danger.

Once at the lake, Henry would back the Ford into the water far enough so we could jump off the back end. Of course, the top was down; the top was always down, except when it looked like rain.

Once we finished swimming, Henry would crank up the T, and we'd all push on the back end to get it out of the water, and we were on our way home.

But the Model T had its problems, as did most cars in those days. It was a hard starter. To start it, you were supposed to advance the spark with the lever on the left side of the steering wheel. The machine operated with a magneto, which provided an electric current to the spark plugs—a system considerably different from those in cars today. And the T did not have an electric starter; you cranked it.

A crank is a bent handle that you stuck into a slot beneath the radiator. It performed the same function that electric starters do today, except a person had to move the crank. Cranking had its dangers, too, for the engine sometimes backfired and sent the crank in the wrong direction, resulting in broken thumbs, wrists, and arms.

With the spark in the upright position and the gas lever advanced a little, you grabbed the crank with your right hand and pulled on a choke wire that stuck out beneath the radiator with your other hand. With a couple twists of the crank, the engine was supposed to start. Sometimes it did. Often it didn't. In winter, the problem was even worse because with cold weather everything was stiff and tight. Sometimes a person would start a fire in a metal container and, when the fire was down to coals, place it under the oil pan of the engine to warm things up. It was a dangerous stunt, but it usually helped.

If the cranking proved futile—which meant you had cranked for fifteen or twenty minutes and your arm felt like it would fall off and your language had taken a turn toward profanity—you gave the front tire a kick and sat down on a stump to think about your alternatives: drive the horses and wagon to town, walk, or consider another alternative for starting that very difficult beast.

Henry was not one to cuss, but when he had cranked his Ford for twenty minutes and he didn't get a "pop" out of it, my brothers and I learned some new language.

Pa had a suggestion. He never said much to Henry about his Model T, but Pa had a lot experience driving those old black cars.

"Let's jack up a back wheel," Pa said.

"I'll try anything," a frustrated Henry said.

The rear end of a Model T isn't all that heavy. Pa found a cedar fence post and a block of wood and levered up the Model T, while Henry put another block of wood under the axle.

Henry screwed on the wheel that was now well off the ground and did manage to get a couple chugs, but it still didn't start.

"Jerry, go fetch the team," Pa said.

I ran off to the barn, harnessed our horses, Frank and Charlie, and drove them over to the where the Model T sat with one of its back wheels off the ground.

"Let's get her back on the ground and hitch the team to her," Pa said.

It was quite a sight—Pa driving the team, Henry at the steering wheel. My brothers and I sat on the back seat as we drove around and around the night pasture until, finally, the occasional chug came more often and the machine began running on its own.

"Never have this problem with horses," Pa said, smiling. "Horses always start."

That fall, when the potatoes were dug and the corn was cut and shocked, we bid goodbye to Henry Lackelt and his Model T. My last memory of Henry was him in his car, heading down the driveway and turning onto the country road. He turned his head, smiled, and waved, and we never saw or heard from Henry Lackelt again.

April Thoughts

~ As I work in my garden, I often stop and smell the newly turned soil. I pick it up in my fingers and reflect on how everything depends on the land—this land and land like it. It is land that feeds the world. But it's taken for granted. And often abused, misused, exploited. How easy it is to forget our connection to the land.

~ Worry is like being stuck in deep mud. The wheels keep turning, but nothing happens.

~ Getting into something is usually easier than getting out of it.

~ On a sunny day in April, I sit on a hillside near some trees. The only sound is that of birds flitting through the still-naked branches. I feel the warm sun on my back, and I breathe deeply the spring air that is filled with the promise of new life. I look for the first hints of green grass and the swelling buds on an old lilac bush. I feel like leaping in the air and yelling "Hooray!"

~ In early April, I glimpse the first bluebird of the season inspecting a birdhouse: checking the accommodations, entering, leaving, entering again, deciding. It is a time for renewal, a time for a new generation of bluebirds to come forth and treat us with the splendor of their color.

~ Remember Earth Day. The first one was April 22, 1970.

~ As we spend time keeping track of our things, our accumulations, our *stuff*, we have less time to keep track of our families, our communities, and ourselves. The best things in life are usually not things.

~ Nobody is making any more land. What we've got is what we've got, so we'd better take care of it.

~ Plant a tree—or two. Nothing speaks louder about your hope for the future. Recall Arbor Day at the country school, when tree planting was often a part of the event. The first Arbor Day was April 10, 1872.

~ I enjoy spending time in the woods, away from the barrier of walls and windows. Among the trees, I am close to nature—a part of it, not apart from it. I go to the woods to think, to clear my mind of the burdens of the day, to cultivate the humbleness that comes from standing among century-old trees. I go to the woods to renew my humanity, to contemplate my place among all nature's creatures.

~ I like to sneak up to a marshy area near my pond on a cool morning as the sun is rising. If I'm fortunate, I might glimpse a male sandhill crane doing a mating dance, impressing his spouse with his acrobatics as he jumps and struts and flaps his six-foot wings. What a sight it is to see this four-foot-tall gray bird with a splotch of red on his forehead showing off to a female, as males have done for generation upon generation.

~ A logger has cut some trees in my white pine wood-lot. I stop and inspect a stump and count the growth

rings—seventy-plus. I think about what was going on in
the world when the tree was a seedling. The Second World
War hadn't yet started. The country was in the throes of the
Great Depression, and farming was difficult. During those
Depression years, acres of farmland suffered from drought,
and the hot summer winds created huge dirty brown dust
clouds. These trees were planted to slow the wind and to
keep the precious topsoil in place.

~ A green haze covers the black willow trees as the little, tightly
curled leaves struggle to unfurl. Reddish brown flowers appear on the maple tree just west of the cabin. I revel in the
excitement that is spring as new life emerges from the dor-
mancy of winter.

~ I enjoy watching for the first dandelions that open with a
splurge of yellow against the brown grass on the south side
of the cabin. I often wonder why the dandelion is cursed by
so many people when it is one of the first plants in spring to
add a little color to an otherwise bleak landscape.

~ I'm in a grove of black locust trees, being careful to avoid the
inch-long and longer spines that will tear at my clothes and
scratch my arms. Black locust is the "Black Bart" of the tree
world, a villain among the more civil species. The canopy
of a locust woodlot is so thick that little grows on the forest
floor—few shrubs, few wildflowers, almost no other tree
species. But black locust wood makes posts for birdhouses
and for fences that are tough as steel. The black locust flowers, creamy white and resembling those of a garden pea (they
are both legumes), are arranged in drooping clusters. Their
sweet smell attracts bees from miles around, so that when
the trees are in bloom, the sound of bees buzzing drowns out

all other sound. Black locust honey is prized by many. Even villains have their good sides.

～ Check the lilac bushes, noting the green buds and expanding purple blossom tips the size of pencil erasers. They are waiting to transform into dark purple, delicate flowers that send forth a sweet smell that hangs heavy in the air on a warm spring evening.

～ Some four-letter words to ponder:
Hope
Wait
Work
Play
Read
Love

～ My son Steve and I cut brush along the trail to the pond on a sunny April morning. Wild turkeys gobble on the hillside to the north. A ruffed grouse drums, sounding like an old two-cylinder John Deere tractor, starting slowly—*boom, boom*—then increasing in speed—*boom, boom, boom, boom*—before stopping and in a few minutes starting again. A mourning dove calls—a beautiful but sorrowful sound. These beautiful gray birds frequent bird feeders yet call from the wild. The first robins of the season sing boldly. Cutting brush is hard work, but physical exercise is good for the body. And the sounds of spring feed the soul.

～ On an early April morning, I stand by my pond, not moving but listening and watching. I see a pair of mallards swimming on the far side, unconcerned until they spot me and lift from the water, the female quacking loudly, protesting my presence. They fly north, then bank west, flying together in formation, the female continuing her protest as they fly over, checking me out, trying to decide if I'm friendly. And then they set their wings, stiffen their legs and set down again on the end of the pond as far from me as they can get. The female ceases her protest, and they resume feeding.

~ In the distance, a Canada goose calls. It is a local, one of those who have chosen to nest here rather than wing their way north to Canada. They take their chances with the foxes and raccoons that raid their nests, and the snapping turtles that come from the depths of the pond and devour little goslings before they've scarcely known life. The honking comes closer, and soon a pair of geese appears just above the treetops to the east, flying north and then west before banking to land, like jet planes lining up for the runway. They spread their wings wide and extend their feet just before they strike the water, slowing down, easing onto the pond with scarcely a sound. The male honks loudly, each honk echoing in the valley around the pond—a strange, eerie, haunting sound. The pair swims toward the center of the pond, ignoring us. And then, from the east, another pair approaches, and they too set their wings and land. But now the newly arrived gander attacks the first male. There is great splashing and honking, while the two females float nearby, watching the strange goings-on. And then the fighting stops, and both pairs swim apart. The anger between the two ganders is probably a form of "you're in my space and I want you out." We humans do the same thing—except our splashing and honking takes different forms.

~ To know what's up ahead, talk to people on their way back.

⤙ Keep an eye on the rhubarb as it quickly pushes out of the ground, bold, fearless of freezing nights, a reminder that spring is truly here. It is time for pie, sauce, and rhubarb crisp from what the old timers called "pie plant" and what Pa called nature's "spring tonic."

RHUBARB CRISP

1 cup flour
3/4 cup oatmeal
1 cup brown sugar
1 teaspoon cinnamon
1/2 cup butter or margarine, softened
1 cup granulated sugar
2 tablespoons cornstarch
1 cup water
1 teaspoon vanilla
4 cups rhubarb, chopped

Mix together the flour, oatmeal, brown sugar, and cinnamon. Add butter or margarine to the flour mixture until crumbly.

Press about half of flour mixture into a 9 x 13-inch greased pan.

Combine granulated sugar and cornstarch in a small saucepan. Add water and vanilla. Cook this sugar-water mixture over medium heat until clear, stirring constantly. Remove from heat.

Add rhubarb to the sugar-water mixture, coating the rhubarb.

Pour rhubarb over crust. Place remaining flour crumbs on top. Bake at 350 degrees for 50 to 60 minutes.

May

An Unhappy Memory

For me, May is the month of an unhappy memory. In 1947, I was twelve years old. A dreaded disease—we called it infantile paralysis at the time, now it's called polio—began marching across the country, striking down city kids, small-town kids, and country kids alike. It wasn't a new disease. President Franklin Delano Roosevelt had contracted it in 1921, and in 1934, Los Angeles had a major outbreak and reported 2,500 cases from May through November at one hospital alone. In 1938, the March of Dimes of the National Foundation for Infantile Paralysis began collecting money to fight the disease. Sister Elizabeth Kenny, in 1940, promoted new procedures—using hot-packing and stretching affected limbs—for treating polio victims.

However, all through World War II, we heard little about polio. Most of us didn't know President Roosevelt was confined to a wheelchair, the result of paralyzed legs from the disease. Of course, we could only hear the president on radio; there was no television, and the newspaper photographers never showed his wheelchair.

After the war, the number of polio cases in the country exploded as people once more began taking vacations, meeting in large groups, and participating in social activities. From 1945 to 1949, more than 20,000 cases were reported each year. In 1952 alone, the national government reported 58,000 cases. From

1950 to 1955, an average of 38,000 cases were reported each year.
For a long time, nobody knew what caused the disease, how it was
transmitted, or how to prevent it. But they knew it passed from
person to person. Fairs were cancelled, swimming beaches closed,
public gatherings suspended. Country people feared going to
town. Children were told to play only with kids they always had
played with.

By 1955, Dr. Jonas Salk and a team of researchers had de-
veloped a vaccine for the polio, which they had discovered was
caused by a virus. With support from March of Dimes funds, mass
immunizations took place, and by the 1960s, only a handful of
polio cases were reported.

One day in spring 1946, we learned that a neighbor boy had contracted infantile paralysis. In a few weeks, he died. A chill went
through our farming community, because now polio wasn't just a
disease that other children got in some faraway city or in another
state. Polio had come to our neighborhood.

During the summer of 1946, we couldn't swim at the public beach at Silver Lake. We reluctantly attended the county fair,
which had remained open. Our country school started that fall
as usual. About the only thing Faith Jenks, our teacher that year,
said was that we should wash our hands more often. Washing our
hands helped to prevent many diseases, not only polio. We didn't
talk about polio, but we all knew about it and got the news when
some other child was stricken. We read about bulbar polio, which
makes breathing, swallowing, and speaking difficult and results in
victims spending time in an iron lung, a hideous-looking machine
that helps them breathe. We learned that the Wild Rose Hospital
had a couple of iron-lung machines. The neighbor boy who died
had bulbar polio.

The other kind of polio, paralytic, caused paralysis in one or
both legs of the victim. Those who survived this type of polio

usually spent their lives in wheelchairs or walking with crutches and canes.

No one wanted polio, no matter what kind. We did our schoolwork and our farm chores, and we looked forward to winter with ice skating, skiing, sledding, and ice fishing. We tried to live our lives as normally as possible, but the cloud of polio hung over everyone. Who would be next?

After the Christmas holidays, we settled into our usual winter routine on the farm. But one day in January, I came home from school with a sore throat. My mother thought I must have been coming down with a cold. She suggested I gargle my throat with warm saltwater and go to bed early. The next morning, the sore throat remained, and I felt miserable. I'd had colds before, and what I had didn't feel like a head cold. Ma felt my forehead and declared I was burning with fever.

"Herm, I think we should take him to the doctor," my mother said to my dad.

Pa, who had grown up during a time when doctors were scarce and people took care of their own health needs, replied, "I think we should wait a day or two, see if he's better."

The next day, I was worse, and my right leg began hurting. It felt like a horse had kicked me or like the time a log slipped and fell on my leg. Nothing would stop the pain. Something new occurred as well: my right knee had a permanent bend and wouldn't move. Try as I might, I couldn't straighten my right leg. With my leg cocked, I couldn't walk, except by dragging myself along with the help of a chair.

That afternoon, we drove to Wild Rose and saw Dr. Hadden at the hospital. He looked me over and checked my leg, which still hurt fiercely.

"Straighten your leg, son," he said.

"I can't," I said, trying to hold back tears.

"Try harder," he instructed.

No matter how hard I tried to straighten my leg, my knee was frozen stiff

Dr. Hadden shook his head.

"What is it?" my mother asked.

"I'm afraid it's infantile paralysis." He had a serious, almost sorrowful, look on his face. "I've seen too many cases of this in the past few months."

"What do we do?" Pa asked.

"Not much you can do," the doctor answered. "Keep him comfortable, have him drink lots of fruit juices, keep him in bed, and let the disease run its course."

"Run its course," my mother said. "What does that mean?"

"Well, first let me say how lucky your son is. He doesn't have bulbar polio, which is usually a killer. I'm quite sure he'll survive. In a few days, the fever will disappear and in a week or so the pain will go away."

"Then what?" Pa asked.

"Your son will probably not be able to use his right leg again."

"Not use his leg? We're farmers. He helps me on the farm."

"Well, not for a good while he won't, if ever," Dr. Hadden said.

As I think back to the session with the doctor and his prognosis of my future, I try to remember what it was like to be twelve years old. Up until my illness, I did much of a man's work on the farm. I drove horses and the tractor. I milked cows and did barn chores. I helped with threshing, silo filling, wood sawing, and all the other jobs that were a part of a family farm operation in those days.

At school, I was on our softball team that played other schools and often won. I could run fast, hit fairly well, and shag long balls when I played in the outfield. If you can't run, you can't play softball.

All these thoughts flashed through my mind as I sat in the back seat of our old 1936 Plymouth on our drive back to the farm. My folks said nothing the entire trip. Pa helped me into the house and onto the bed they had made up for me in the dining room, where I would be close to the woodstove. Ma bought several cans of fruit juice, orange and grapefruit. She opened a can of grapefruit juice and poured it into a glass for me. It was awful—sour-tasting and milky white in appearance.

"I hate this stuff," I said.

"Doctor said you must drink it," Ma said.

"I still hate it. Tastes bad."

"Drink it," Pa said. He wasn't smiling. So I drank it.

By early March, when the snow began melting and the Canada geese were winging north, I was able to sit up and had regained some of my strength. The pain and fever had disappeared, but my right knee remained frozen and the only way I could walk was to push a chair in front of me or lean heavily on a cane. The way my leg was cocked, only my toe hit the floor, and the leg didn't have enough strength to support me.

I was in eighth grade at Chain O' Lake country school, and already I had missed several weeks. My mother contacted Mrs. Jenks, and she agreed to bring schoolwork out to the farm so that I could work on it each day. Pa made a desk for me out of orange crates. In those days, oranges were delivered to the stores in wooden boxes with two compartments. Pa stood two orange crates on end and nailed a board across the top. Thus I had a fine desk with a shelf on each side where I could keep my schoolbooks.

Each day after school, Mrs. Jenks drove to the farm, brought me my day's assignments, and picked up what I had worked on. She also took time to answer any questions I had about the assignments. To move from elementary school to high school, all eighth-grade students had to sit for a day of examinations at the county courthouse. The country superintendent of schools office gave examinations for math, social studies, geography, history, science, and even penmanship. Mrs. Jenks, Ma and Pa, and I knew that to have any chance of going to high school the next year, I had to pass the county exams.

Now it was early April, and I was feeling sorry for myself and moping around the house, complaining about all the schoolwork I had to do, and resisting the ever-present fruit juice that Ma made me drink. I had no appetite, and I had become a skinny little skeleton.

"When can I quit drinking this miserable canned fruit juice?" I asked.

"Doctor said to keep drinking it." We had returned to the doctor several times and he had said I was making good progress. But when I asked him about my leg and when I would be able to run again, he didn't answer. All he would say was, "You're coming along fine." We kept hearing about other children who had contacted the disease and died or were far more paralyzed than I was.

By early April, when field work was starting, Pa said maybe I could help by driving the tractor on the disk. "I can't drive the tractor. I can't do anything," I whined. "I can't even walk."

"You just have to sit on the seat and steer," he said. "Your arms work, don't they?"

"Yes, my arms work."

On a warm April day, Pa lifted me onto the seat of our Farmall H tractor that he had hitched to the disk harrow. He rode on the tractor with me out to the field in front of the house, twenty acres where he would plant oats. I, of course, had disked oat ground before; in fact, I rather enjoyed doing it. But could I operate the tractor with a bad leg? I could push in the clutch, which required my left leg. But the brakes were on the other side, and my right leg, in its cocked position, couldn't even reach them.

I had several close calls. I ran into the wire fence one time and almost hit a big stone another time, all because I couldn't use the brakes. But after a week of tractor driving, my appetite came back and my leg had straightened enough so that I could use the brakes a little.

It was interesting therapy. Force your leg to work or the tractor will run into something. Pa was grumpy the whole time. Whenever I said I couldn't drive the tractor, after I had wiped out a couple fence posts and tangled the disk in barbwire, he just said, "Keep going. We've got lots of work to do."

No sympathy at all. No concern. But I was wrong in thinking he was grumpy. He knew what needed to be done. He knew that my knee would never work unless I gave it a chance, and what better physical therapy than having to use the brakes on the tractor when you were headed downhill and about to run into a wire fence?

By the end of April, I could hobble along with a serious limp. Now I was back in school each day. Pa took me to school with the car for the first week, but then said I should be able to walk. After all, it was only a mile each way. And walk I did. Before I was sick, I could walk to school in fifteen or twenty minutes. Now it took me more than a half hour of limping down the dusty road.

Mrs. Jenks said I should plan to play softball. When I told her that I couldn't run—she, of course, knew that—she said I could be the pitcher.

"Pitchers don't have to run much," she said. So I became the pitcher. I had a great incentive to pitch well, to strike out as many kids as I could, because if the ball came bouncing back toward the pitcher's mound and I tried to pick it up, I would likely fall on my face. This, of course, happened, and the other team members laughed at me for being such a stumblebum.

We all face turning points in our lives—events that occur, often through no cause of our own, and dramatically affect what we do and what we become. Polio had such an effect on my life. I passed my eighth-grade exams, thanks to Mrs. Jenks, and started high school in 1947, but I couldn't play baseball or basketball or participate in track. My high school teachers were understanding—much more so in retrospect than I thought at the time. Mr. Wright, who coached three sports, asked if I would announce the basketball games. So while my classmates were running up and down the floor, I sat on the sidelines describing to the audience what was happening and learning how to use a microphone. Another teacher, Mr. Harvey, supervised the monthly school newspaper, the *Rosebud*, and suggested I work on it. I worked my way up from assistant editor to editor. We used L. C. Smith manual typewriters and a hectograph (a machine that predated mimeograph machines) to produce the paper. I wrote a monthly editorial and I wrote about school happenings—certainly not literature, but I was learning how to string words together. I learned how to type and how to write.

From the time I first came down with polio, I began reading books, one after the other. When I was sick, relatives brought me books—fiction and nonfiction, classics and contemporary works. My love of reading continued all through high school and college and has never diminished.

As awful as the experience was, especially as it gave me a sense of worthlessness on the farm, polio caused me to do what my father always said: "Do the best you can with what you've got."

May Thoughts

～ I remember May baskets, homemade paper baskets that we made in school and filled with spring flowers. We hung them on a neighbor's door, yelled "May basket," then ran with the hope the youngsters inside would chase us and catch us and join up as we walked to the next neighbor to repeat the spring ritual. With neighbors more than half mile apart, the evening was more walking than hanging baskets.

～ Do nothing in haste, except running away from an angry dog.

～ As I walk toward a small field where I have planted oats, rye, and an assortment of other crops for the wildlife, I startle a wild turkey hen that sees me about the same time I see her. She is scratching in the newly planted oat field. Impatient. Not willing to wait for the oats to grow and ripen. She gallops off like a long-legged racehorse and then, unsatisfied with the distance she is creating by running, flaps her enormous wings and lifts over the black locust patch to the west. Like a 747 airliner of the bird world, the giant turkey disappears over the treetops, her wings flapping effortlessly.

～ I stand on a hill above the pond and watch the wind play with the surface of the water, creating swirls and circles, sending little waves rolling up on the shore, washing the rocks before receding. I think about the wind and its art, which we seldom stop to observe in our hurry to do what seems so important at the time, but usually isn't.

⌁ Oh, how I enjoy a rainy spring night, when thunder rumbles in the distance and raindrops splatter against the bedroom window, making sleep come easy.

⌁ On a warm day in May, I gaze at a long, tree-covered hillside to the west of the cabin. Birch, aspen, maple, and oak of several varieties grow there. I am in awe of the display of greens from light to dark, from quiet to bold. The hillside shows a diversity of green, a palate of subtle shades. Nature celebrates spring in the woods, before the dark and uniform greens of summer take over.

⌁ On an early May morning, as the sun lifts over the pines to the east, I listen to the birdsong. Robins and orioles. Grosbeaks and song sparrows. Migrants who have returned and are talking it up. They celebrate spring with song and flashes of color. Building nests. Laying eggs. In a hurry after their winter rest in a warmer place.

⌁ After the sun has slipped away and the last robin has sung its evening song, I listen for the spring peepers, those tiny frogs, no longer than an inch or so, who sing in unison. To the unknowing, they sound like birds chirping. They sing from the shrubs and trees overhanging the water. They sing with such enthusiasm that their sound drowns out all early evening sound. They sing of spring, confirming its arrival.

⌁ On a day when I had wanted to work outside, had bought garden seeds and made plans, I woke up to rain—slow, steady, drippy, soaking rain. It's hard not to be disappointed. But the weather is nature's way of reminding me who is in charge, who makes the big decisions. The rain put me in my place.

~ I've planted a vegetable garden every year for more than forty years. It gives me a chance to get down on my knees and dig. To dirty my hands. To smell freshly worked soil. To pinch it between my fingers and look at it closely. To feel the connection that we all have to the land. And to teach my grandchildren how to plant pumpkin seeds.

~ I recall my father's words, "Rain in May is a barn full of hay," as raindrops drum against the kitchen window and the day's outdoor plans are revised. The grass seems to leap out of the ground with the moisture that has been slow in coming. And the hayfields, too, are greening up and growing, promising a good haying season.

~ Garden thoughts:

Plant one kernel of sweet corn for the table, one for the crow, and one for dry weather.

Grow a garden, and you'll always have something to eat.

If rabbits insist on eating your green beans, plant a few more hills.

Grow at least one row of rutabagas.

An eggplant's beauty exceeds its taste. A garden is one kind of miracle.

Gardening keeps one humble. As much as we try to control what happens with carefully selected seeds, proper weed control, even periodic watering, gardens still constantly surprise us with what grows and what doesn't.

~ An old apple tree grows south of the cabin, the sole survivor of a small orchard. Each spring, it bursts forth with pink blossoms that have a delicate and special aroma. I examine a single blossom and note how beautiful yet fragile it is. I enjoy the tree for several days, and then it rains. The petals, like newly fallen snow, cluster under the tree, reminders of what they once were.

~ Slow down on dark, rainy days. Dawdle over a second cup of coffee. Read parts of the newspaper you usually skip. Listen to classical music on the public radio station. A rainy morning is nature's way of interrupting the headlong rush that seems to be the fate for most of us.

~ Find joy in simple things. The sight of the first bluebird in spring. A hawk soaring in a cloudless sky. The gobble of a wild turkey at sunrise. A rainbow that stretches from horizon to horizon. A drink of cool well water. The first radish from the garden each spring. A dark, moonless night filled with millions of stars.

~ On a warm May evening, I go fishing with my brother Don. We fish on a small lake where we are the only fishermen, floating in my old Sears aluminum boat, while red-winged blackbirds scold from their perches near shore and a pair of Canada geese with a nest nearby raises a ruckus at our presence. Fishing soon becomes secondary as we both recall fishing this lake when we were little boys. We remember the fish being bigger and the lake larger. Such is the stuff of fish stories and brotherly reminiscence.

~ With my grandsons, I walk along the edge of my pond, which once held water but is now dry land. New paper birch trees have sprung up in the sandy, moist soil. A hundred of them, maybe more, each about two feet tall, have new leaves sneaking out on slender branches, getting a head start before the shore grass catches hold and grows as tall as they are. The birch trees will struggle the entire summer, competing for light and nutrients; some will lose the battle and die. But those that survive will have grown enough so the following year they will be taller than any competing grass, and they will be on their way—until the pond water level climbs high enough to cover both the grass and the birches.

Every year I plant a row of broom corn in my garden, the kind that has no ears but sends up coarse spikes with seeds at the end. When it's ripe in the fall, I show my grandkids how brooms are made, how to remove the seeds, gather the brown spikes—broom stalks—into a bunch, and wire them together to make a broom. I try to impress upon the grandkids that this is a real broom that began when I planted a little seed in the ground in the spring.

Sometimes, when I am eating lunch, I watch a pair of red squirrels scavenge under the bird feeder. The little squirrels fight over the leavings, leap on each other, scold, try to chase each other away. As the squirrels squabble, a pair of blue jays and then later a brilliantly red cardinal contentedly eat at the feeder, ignoring what is going on beneath them.

With May soon gone, I remember the end-of-school-year picnic at our country school. All the families with children at the school gathered in the schoolyard, and we ate a potluck dinner topped off with ice cream that the school board purchased for the occasion. Each year, the schoolchildren played against their fathers in softball. The day was special, because for most of us, it was one of the few times we saw our fathers play.

June

Ginger

One early June evening, when the day's work was finished, Pa, my brothers, and I were sitting on the back porch resting. We heard a truck coming along our dirt road some distance away. Soon we saw it, a huge cloud of dust rolling up the road behind it. The truck slowed for our driveway and turned in.

"Ross Caves," Pa said. "I wonder why he's coming this time of day?" A hint of a smile spread across Pa's tanned face. Caves was the local livestock trucker who lived in Wild Rose and regularly picked up calves, pigs, and cows and hauled them to the stockyards in Milwaukee. When he was making a pickup, he generally came in the morning, so he had time for the trip to Milwaukee.

A cloud of dust from the driveway swirled around the red truck as it came to a halt. Our collie farm dog, Fanny, barked a couple of times to announce that someone had arrived. Then she went back to dozing on the porch. She had seen the Caves truck many times before, so there was little need to display her watchdog duties.

"Hello, Herm," Ross said as he climbed down from the cab. "This a good place to unload?"

"Sure," Pa answered. Then he turned to my brothers and me. "We might need some help. Come on over here." He was smiling.

Now I was really curious. What could Ross Caves be delivering to our farm? Pa must have purchased a new cow or calf from somewhere, I thought. Caves let down the loading platform and fastened the side panels in place, making a loading chute from the truck to the ground.

"Come on up here, boys," Caves said. "Have a look."

I was eight years old; Don and Darrel were five. Never before had we been invited up the loading chute into the truck. It was considered too dangerous, particularly when there was livestock in the vehicle. Farm animals, docile and quiet one moment, could turn violent and dangerous another, particularly when they were being transported. "What do you think, Jerry?" Ross said as he pointed to the animal tied to a side wall of the truck.

"It's a pony," I said. "Whose is it?"

"Far as I know, he belongs to you boys."

"It's ours?" I said, scarcely able to believe what I was seeing. Once or twice I had mentioned how much fun it would be to have a pony, but Pa always reminded me that we didn't enough money to make ends meet. A pony was a luxury we could not afford.

"Does he kick?" my brother Darrel asked.

"Nah, he doesn't kick," Caves said. "He's as tame as a puppy dog." Caves untied the rope from the side of the truck and handed it to me. The little brown Shetland pony followed along behind me, down the chute and onto the grass. Later I learned that the pony had spent his lifetime getting in and out of trucks, as he had been a performing pony for a circus. The circus truck had been in a wreck, and the pony's knees were injured, so he was no longer able to perform. Clarence Hurst, who lived in Wild Rose, bought the pony from the circus when it traveled through our area. Hurst thought my brothers and I might enjoy a pony, so he asked Pa if he'd like to buy him. They agreed on fifteen dollars, which included a badly worn and too large rope halter.

"What'll we name him?" I asked excitedly. I tried to think of pony names—Rex, Brownie (the pony was brown with a patch of white on his forehead), Flash, Dynamite (I'd never heard a pony called by that name, but it sounded exciting).

"He's already named," Caves said. "His name is Ginger." Upon hearing his name, the pony looked toward Caves, his alert ears pointed forward.

"Guess he knows his name," Caves said. "Well, I gotta be going," he said as he climbed back into the cab of the truck. "Have fun with your pony."

"No riding Ginger until tomorrow," Pa said, anticipating my question. "Help me find a place for him in the barn."

We made a little stall for Ginger next to the calf pen in the far corner of the barn, wiring a metal ring to the wall where we could tie him. While we were milking the cows that night, I slipped over to Ginger's stall and petted him on the neck. My brothers also were petting the pony and talking about all the things they were going to do now that we had Ginger. I couldn't go to sleep that night, thinking about our pony and all the wonderful things that we would do together. We could play cowboy, and it would be genuine—no running around with a stick dragging between our legs making believe that it was a horse. Ginger was real.

The next morning, when the chores were done, Pa brought out a shiny new leather bridle that the harness maker in Wild Rose had made. It was brown and had a silver-colored circle on each side. Pa had kept the bridle hidden from us, wanting the pony to be a surprise. There was no money for a saddle, so we rode bareback, taking turns as Pa led Ginger around the yard.

Soon we were riding Ginger without Pa's assistance, sometimes as far as the neighbor's, a mile or more away. Ginger, like most farm animals, had a special personality. He soon knew me and my two brothers very well. When Darrel rode him, Ginger's favorite trick was to walk under a low-hanging apple tree branch and brush Darrel off. Darrel would pick himself up from the ground and run after the escaping pony, shaking his fist.

Pa helped us make a harness for the pony out of scrap pieces of leather we found around the farm. For tugs—the part of the harness that attaches to an implement—Pa showed us how to braid binder twine. Between the house and the barn was a little sandy area, maybe ten feet square, where my brothers and I played. We laid out fields with store-string fences and sometimes planted oats or corn, like Pa did in the farm fields. We called this place the "sand hole."

Donald was always inventing new things to do with Ginger. One day—he must have been seven or eight at the time—he harnessed up Ginger and hooked the tugs to a one-horse cultivator, the kind Pa used to cultivate the garden, the cucumber patch, and the potato field. When Ginger, Don, and the cultivator arrived at the sand hole, Don lifted up the cultivator; the handles in the upright position stood about as tall as he did. Ginger could pull the cultivator fairly easily when it was dragging on its side and not working, but when the cultivator shovels dug in, he couldn't. He pulled with all his might, but he didn't have the strength to pull the cultivator in its working position.

"Giddap," Don said, doing what he'd seen Pa do many times when our team of horses was in a tough pulling situation. The little pony dug in and strained, and the binder-twine tugs broke. That was the end of Don's cultivating adventure.

As the years passed, Ginger gained complete freedom around the farm. He and Fanny became close buddies. The two of them wandered around the farm at will. We often heard from a neighbor passing by, "Did you know your pony was out?"

The dog and the pony went for the cows together. It was a strange sight—a dog and a pony walking down the farm lane with our herd of Holstein cows strung out before them. Of course, it was the dog's job to retrieve the cows from the pasture each morning and afternoon. She took her friend along for company. When we were in the hayfield bunching freshly raked hay, the pony and the dog were along. As we stood oat bundles in shocks, prior to threshing, the pony and the dog accompanied us. Everywhere Fanny went, Ginger was along.

One fall, when we were digging potatoes and Ginger was in the potato field watching us, he swallowed a potato, which became lodged in his throat. Pa tried everything to dislodge it, but nothing worked. We called the veterinarian, but he said there was nothing we could do aside from surgery. By now, Ginger was quite old as ponies go, and the surgery was high risk and costly. The potato remained in place, and soon we realized there was nothing we could do for Ginger.

My brothers and I took turns staying with the dying pony as he lay in his little stall in the barn, next to the calf pen. Fanny was there, too, never leaving his side.

Within two days, our beloved Ginger was dead. We buried the pony in a special place, in the shade of a white pine windbreak on the west side of the farm. We made a little cross out of two pine branches tied together with binder twine. When the grave was filled with dirt and the cross firmly placed, Pa, Fanny, my brothers, and I all stood for a few minutes, saying nothing. We all were crying. Pa was trying to hide it, but he couldn't. Finally he blew his nose and said, "Well, that's it." We all walked slowly home, saying nothing.

June Thoughts

⌁ I marvel at the patience of black locust trees. They are the last to leaf out in the spring, even later than the oaks. Their patience pays off. By waiting, the locust trees avoid late frosts. I think about the value of patience in our lives. How often we hurry to do something when waiting might be the better choice, helping us to avoid serious problems that often result from haste.

⌁ In early June, I constantly check my garden to see which seeds have germinated and which have not. It's not too late to fill in the missing places with new seeds, even though there is nothing wrong with a few empty spaces in the garden.

⌁ If you are the father of the bride, keep your mouth shut and your wallet open.

⌁ When people say bad things about you, live so nobody will believe them.

⌁ It's all right to not have anything to say as long as you don't say it.

⌁ On a rainy day, I watch raindrops create little circles on the pond. The circles quickly expand, run into each other, disappear, and are immediately replaced by others. I think about how our lives are like that. We make a little splash; it disappears and is replaced by someone else's splash. The splashes come and go, but the surface of the pond ultimately changes little.

~ June is for listening to birdsong at sunrise—warbles and whistles, chirps and extended melodies, caws and gobbles from robins, cardinals, grosbeaks, catbirds, chickadees, Baltimore orioles, finches, crows, and wild turkeys and, at the pond, the eerie, historic call of the sandhill crane. The birds create a litany of music, each one performing its own special song. Except for the catbird, which mimics the songs of other birds, confusing the listener as to the tune's source.

~ When worry overtakes me, I take up a hoe and head for the garden. Nothing takes my mind away from troubled thoughts faster than chopping out weeds and clearing the way for the vegetables to grow.

~ Plant your corn when the leaves of the oak are the size of a mouse's ear.

~ When I'm driving along a quiet country road, I often stop when I come upon a field of newly mown hay. I enjoy smelling freshly cut alfalfa and clover. A smell different from all others. Unique to the rural landscape. Special. Nothing like it anywhere else.

~ When the sun creeps below the trees to the west, I hoe weeds from the potatoes in my garden. I feel a great sense of accomplishment as I deliberately move down the row, turning up weed-free soil and leaving the potatoes to grow without competition. The immediate payoff is the sight of brown soil against lush, green potato plants; the future payoff is homegrown potatoes on my dinner plate.

⟿ Today I'm searching for a special butterfly as I stand in a patch of purple and blue lupines, their flowers carpeting the ground. I'm looking for a tiny Karner blue butterfly that depends on the lupine for its existence. The Karner blue is an endangered species. It is no larger than my little fingernail, yet its flitting from flower to flower provides an alert observer with the treat of seeing something that is rare and strikingly beautiful. I encourage the growth of the lupines, for in their survival rests the future of this tiny butterfly.

⟿ A neighbor grows "pick yourself"' strawberries. On a dewy sunny morning, I pick several quarts. I look forward to Ruth's strawberry pie—an annual treat!

⟿ On a rainy day, I think about the old adage, "Rain in June is a silver spoon." I ponder its meaning and then take the day off and go fishing.

⟿ On an early foggy morning, I watch a pair of Canada geese emerge from the mists on the pond with three little goslings in tow. A fourth hangs back, trying to hide in the rushes until its mother turns around and urges the little maverick to join the rest. No matter what the species, it seems one youngster always has a mind of its own and requires extra attention from its mother.

⟿ I enjoy hiking in my white pine woodlot on a rainy morning. I stop and listen to the subtle, gentle sound of raindrops on pine needles. And I smell the richness of pine hanging heavy in the damp air.

⟿ I pull a plump, red radish from my garden, snap off the top, rub the root against my pant leg to remove the soil, admire the radish's vivid color, and then pop it into my mouth. Radishes are my first garden crop of the year—the miracle of seed to vegetable takes just a matter of days. I pull a bunch of them, leaving on the tops. I hand them to Ruth with a smile.

~ I remember what it was like when, as a kid, I climbed the ladder in the haymow of our barn and looked out the little window at the top. Everything looked different when I was forty feet above it. For many things in life, one's perspective can change when you climb above the fray and look down at it.

~ As I work in my garden, I think about the thousands of newly emerging weeds I'm eliminating. The vegetables and the weeds all compete for the same sunlight, the same moisture, and the same nutrients. For the garden plants to succeed, they need my help. I realize that for each of us to succeed we also need assistance, someone to help clear the way so we can grow.

~ In June, I patiently watch for the lupines to green up and begin thrusting forth delicate blue flowers. The flower is misnamed, as *lupine* comes from *Lupus*, Latin for "wolf." Lupines were once thought to steal from the soil, as the wolf searches for its prey. But the opposite is true; the lupine is a soil builder, a giver, not a taker. It is a legume, which adds fertility to the soil.

~ On a foggy morning, I watch five wild turkeys feed, oblivious to being watched, but alert and attentive nonetheless. Near the turkeys, a whitetail doe, with her fawn, eats. The little one, on springy legs, occasionally leaps playfully into the air, while the mother ignores it and continues feeding on the lush valley grass. The turkeys disregard the goings-on.

~ As my grandsons and I walk in the field near the oak woods, we look for little oak trees, tiny and fragile, apt to be eaten by a hungry deer or rabbit or crowded out by faster growing aspen. I compare the little oaks with their sturdy parents—tall, tough, and resilient. Like the little oaks, we each need nurturing in our lives when we are young, so our potential can be expressed and our uniqueness displayed.

~ "What will the neighbors think?" There is no more powerful incentive for a gardener or a farmer than those words. It leads to straight rows, replanting where seeds haven't germinated, and excessive weed control taking more hours of hoeing than is necessary.

~ Sometimes the best thing to do is to go fishing. Take your children or grandchildren with you. Work can wait for another day. Sit in a boat and watch red and white bobbers rise and fall as a spring breeze sifts over the water. Think about earlier fishing days, when you were a kid and were with your father. Recall what your father said: "Fishing is always good, no matter if you catch anything or not."

~ A thunderstorm builds in the west, black clouds tumbling over each other, the thunder rumbling, lightning flashing occasionally. I watch and listen as the storm quickly approaches. The lightning flashes brighter; the thunder booms louder. I feel the extreme quiet just before the storm arrives, not a leaf moving, not a blade of grass waving. Then a gush of cold air slaps my face, and simultaneously there is a brilliant flash of lightning, a blast of thunder, and raindrops the size of dimes splatter in the dry dirt. Awesome!

~ I catch a pail of rainwater from the eaves on a rainy night. My mother prized the rainwater, which was "soft" compared to the well water that was filled with minerals. Soft water was used for washing one's hair, for washing fragile cottons, for watering the potted geraniums.

STRAWBERRY PIE

4 cups (1 quart) fresh strawberries
1 1/2 cups water
1/2 cup sugar
2 tablespoons cornstarch
1 package strawberry gelatin
Graham cracker pie crust, baked (store bought
or make your own)

Wash and hull strawberries. Cut large ones in half. Set aside.

Place water in 2-quart saucepan. Mix sugar and cornstarch together and add to the water. Cook over medium heat until mixture comes to a boil. Cook for 2 minutes, stirring constantly until the mixture is thick and clear. Remove from heat.

Add strawberry gelatin. Stir until gelatin is dissolved.

Coat the berries with the gelatin mixture, and then pour into baked crust.

Chill in the refrigerator until set.

July

The Fourth at Silver Lake

When I was a kid, the Fourth of July was a special day—or at least half of the day was. The Fourth always fell smack in the middle of haying season. Haying in those days meant cutting hayfields with a horse-drawn mower, raking the newly mown hay into long ropes with a horse-pulled dump rake, forking the hay into bunches, and then hauling the hay to the barn on a hay wagon. Without fail, the Fourth of July fell on the day when hay was supposed to be hauled to the barn. No farmer would leave bunched hay in the field; if it rained, the crop would spoil. No matter what—Fourth of July, birth of a new child—hay came first.

I remember one Fourth of July well. Pa didn't mention the holiday when he hitched our team to the hay wagon that morning. My two brothers and I crawled on the wooden wagon rack, and we headed for the hayfield. My brothers and I knew it was the Fourth, and we had saved our money for firecrackers (they were legal in those days). We had little lady fingers, about an inch or so long, and some big crackers, a couple inches long and an inch or so in diameter—the kind that would propel a tin can twenty feet in the air or burst a mailbox door wide open.

We didn't talk about the holiday but bounced out to the field, dangling our legs off the sides of the steel-wheeled hay wagon. Pa was intent on hauling hay as we watched an ominous bank of clouds build in the southwest. After we had hauled two loads of hay to the barn—there was maybe one big load left when we returned to the field—we heard the first rumble of thunder.

"Just what we don't need right now," Pa said as we pitched bunch after bunch of alfalfa and clover hay on the wagon. The first drops of rain splattered on the dry country road as the overfilled wagon slowly creaked its way to the ramp leading into the upper section of the barn.

The team and loaded wagon inside the barn, a bright flash of lightning cut across the roiling black sky, and thunder roared so that that the team jumped.

"Let's wait for a little before we unload," Pa said.

Rain pounded on the barn roof, echoing inside the haymow and pouring off the roof in cascades. It was like being inside a drum while the drummer gently beat a tune above you—a natural, penetrating song that rose and fell. Our farm was sandy, and sandy soil needs lots of rain. Hearing the rain pound on the barn roof meant the harvested hay fields would once more begin growing and perhaps give us a substantial second crop. The ever-thirsty cow pastures would green up and keep growing as well.

Soon the thundershower passed, the sun came out, and we finished unloading the hay. So far, Pa had said nothing about it being the Fourth of July. My brothers and I wondered if Pa was thinking about going to Silver Lake, as we had done for several years on the afternoon of the Fourth. When I was growing up, farm kids never asked their parents, especially their fathers, about their plans. A kid's life was filled with wondering and guessing.

Silver Lake was about six miles east of our farm. It had a wonderful public swimming beach and a resort where city people spent time on vacation. Of course, for my family, there was no such thing as a vacation where you traveled someplace and stayed in a cottage and fished and swam in a lake and did little of anything else. Our vacation, such as potato vacation, when we had two weeks off from school and picked potatoes every day, was no vacation at all. And even Christmas vacation, which also was time off from school, still meant helping with the farm chores like you did every other day of the year. The idea of taking a vacation in summer, when farm work was at its peak, was absolutely unheard of and scoffed at by Pa.

"Those city folks don't know how to work," Pa would say, referring to some of Ma's city relatives who showed up at the farm regularly, mostly just to sidle up to the dining room table and fill themselves up with Ma's good cooking.

As we ate our noon meal, with the sun shining brightly and the rainstorm well off to the east, my brothers and I still wondered about the afternoon. Had Pa forgotten it was the Fourth? Would he suggest we fix fence? This was a common task when it was too wet to do much of anything else.

Finally, Pa pushed back from the table. "Might as well go to Silver Lake and celebrate the Fourth," he said, smiling. These were the words we wanted to hear. Of course, Ma knew all along of Pa's plans and had worked all morning preparing a picnic supper. Into a basket she packed potato salad made from new red potatoes that she covered with slices of cooked eggs. She included cold chicken, apple pie, homemade bread spread thick with butter, banana cake, peanut butter cookies, homemade dill pickles—the works.

It was a kind of holiday conspiracy between Pa and Ma—perhaps Pa's idea of humor, we never knew. We gathered up our remaining firecrackers and our faded and worn swimming trunks. We climbed into the back of our 1936 Plymouth and rumbled off to Silver Lake. Once there, my brothers and I ran off to the bathhouse, a little building where you paid a dime to get a basket for your clothes and the right to change in a little closetlike space with a door that was open on the top and bottom and could be hooked so that some girl wouldn't yank it open and see you standing there bare naked. None of us wanted a girl to see us bare naked, although I thought the opposite might be kind of interesting because we had no sisters. Pa said it was outrageous to pay ten cents for a bath, but we did it only once a year; the rest of the time we went swimming for free. We swam mostly in Chain O' Lake, which was only a mile and a half from our farm. Chain O' Lake's bottom was cluttered with weeds, and we usually attracted bloodsuckers (leeches) when we swam there. We always brought a saltshaker with us to rid ourselves of these black, slimy pests. If a bloodsucker was stuck on your toe, a few sprinkles of salt on the bloodthirsty creature would make it let go and dry up. Of course, what we feared most, and kidded each other about, was having a bloodsucker attach itself to a rather private part of our anatomy. I don't recall that such a thing ever happened, but the prospect was always there.

With our bathing suits on, we ran across the naturally sandy beach and plunged into the clear blue waters of Silver Lake. There were no weeds or bloodsuckers. Silver Lake had slides in the water, both short and tall, and a fancy raft for diving. We tried it all, making sure that we got our ten cents worth.

Around four o'clock, we returned to the bathhouse, changed our clothes, and found Ma and Pa sitting near a picnic table in the shade of a big white pine tree. We shot off our remaining firecrackers while Ma laid out our picnic supper. We ate until we could eat no more.

Finally, Pa said, "Time to go home. Cows don't know it's the Fourth of July."

Back home, we did the evening chores and turned the cows out to pasture. We then gathered on the front porch of the house. We were hoping to glimpse some fireworks, which we could do if there was no wind and it was a clear night.

"There's one," Ma said, pointing to some streaks of blue and red over the treetops to the east. "And there's another, and another."

It had been a grand Fourth of July. Tomorrow it was back to farm work all day.

July Thoughts

~ Enjoy freshly picked leaf lettuce from the garden.

~ On an early evening when the shadows are long, I watch a pair of sandhill cranes near my pond; the female is a bit smaller and grayer than the brown male. They walk along the edge of the water, occasionally in it, bringing up long strands of water weeds from the pond's bottom. Behind them a few feet, its fuzzy head bobbing above the shore grass, is their yet-to-feather little one, trying to keep up with its parents. A sandhill crane family out for an evening stroll, parents introducing their offspring to the ways of the wild and the need to constantly search for food—a major activity for all things wild and not so wild.

~ Sometimes I think about the straightness of our lives: straight walls, straight roads, straight lines, and straight thinking. When I go for a walk, I notice curves and twists and spirals in the outdoors. There are few straight lines in a woodlot, a hillside of wildflowers, a wild grass prairie, a bird nest, a badger den. How does the artificial straightness of our lives affect how we think, how we act, how we see, and what we hear? How does straightness influence our expectations and what we believe is right and what is wrong? What can we learn from the curves and circles and spirals of nature?

∾ A pocketful of common sense is worth a wagonload of learning.

∾ Don't forget the importance of a good example.

∾ Stop to look at a wild daisy. Daisies stand straight and tall, their yellow centers and delicate white petals adding a splash of color to their surroundings. Daisies are eaten, trod upon, sliced off, and beaten back, but they always return, tall and sturdy and in full color. No complaints. No excuses.

∾ There's a lot of talk these days but little being said.

∾ In early evening, Ruth and I often sit in the shade of a big black willow tree that grows in the windbreak west of the cabin. Its bark is thick and rough; its limbs are bent and torn, some mere stubs where the wind has cracked off huge hunks. But the tree, along with its neighboring black willows, has served us well for many years. The willows have kept the winter winds from rattling the cabin windows, prevented snow from piling in the farmyard, and provided a shady resting place, as they do now.

∾ In our attempt to explain everything in nature, we sometimes lose sight of what cannot be explained, what forever will remain a mystery. Why can't we see the wind? How does a red cardinal learn how to whistle? Why is each snowflake different from every other? Why are no two sunsets the same? It is the mystery of the unexplained that adds richness to our lives.

∾ A piece of land has few friends. Most land has a history of exploitation, starting with those who first tilled it, planted it, and harvested its bounty. Or worse, the land was bulldozed, the hills leveled, the hollows filled. Then it was paved with concrete, its identity buried beneath the bright lights of yet another shopping mall or another condominium.

~ On a hot muggy night, when heat lightning flashes across a menacing bank of clouds to the west, I watch fireflies in the field south of the cabin, flashing on and off, on and off, here, there, not predictable, no pattern or plan. Some have said it is a mating ritual. We humans like plans, like things predictable, and so I watch in amazement at these random flashlights that skitter about, making light for an instant and disappearing seemingly without purpose.

~ With the sun down and the shadows of night creeping up the hill from the hollow, I listen to the whippoorwill repeating its name over and over and over. A shy bird, the whippoorwill is seldom seen, but its call is unmistakable. An old wives' tale would have it that if a whippoorwill lights near your doorstep at night and sings, bad luck will follow. The only bad luck may be for the urban person who has never heard a whippoorwill and is robbed of sleep.

~ On a rainy day, I clean off the workbench in the machine shed. I don't remember when last I did this, but I joyfully find so many things that I had forgotten I owned or thought for sure were lost forever—a favorite hammer, a 3/8-inch socket for my socket wrenches, directions for making a bluebird house, two rolls of duct tape, assorted bolts, screws, nuts and washers, nails of various sizes, two never-used paintbrushes, a packet of sandpaper, directions for using the lawnmower I no longer have, an unknown part from the International tractor I sold four years ago, and a garbage bag full of other things once thought important.

∿ Although they often speak pessimistic words, there is no group more optimistic than farmers. Each spring they till the earth and plant seeds, never knowing if they will get a crop because they have no control over the weather, which ultimately makes all the difference for a successful season or not.

∿ Tall trees don't always provide the most shade.

∿ Why do the cows always break out of their pasture when everyone is dressed for church and you were late last week because the same thing happened?

∿ What a mystical experience it is to watch a full moon at midnight, when long eerie shadows slither across the land and an owl's call echoes in the valley.

∿ Every job has its own way of doing, its own rhythm, whether it is digging potatoes with a six-tine fork, pitching hay on a hot, humid day, or adding long columns of numbers in your account book. Once you've found the rhythm, the job becomes easier, sometimes even pleasurable.

∿ Sunsets are for contemplating, as night slowly comes and the day creatures rest and the creatures of the night awaken. It is a time for consolidating in our minds the activities of the day as we look forward to tomorrow, when we can begin fresh and new.

∿ What you think is right may not be what your neighbor thinks is right. There is always the possibility, as remote as it may seem, that you may be wrong.

∿ Why do we praise light and fear darkness? After all, we need darkness to appreciate light, just as we need winter to appreciate summer. Are there deeper reasons for dreading darkness? A concern that we want others to see our bright side and not the dark tendencies that we all have?

~ On a day when the temperature and the humidity are both above ninety, when sweat darkens my shirt and wets my hair, I take a nap after my noon meal—an extended nap in the shade of the big maple tree by the back porch. The work will be there when I wake up.

~ On a cool, rainy morning at the pond, when wisps of fog rise from the water and swallows skim the surface, searching for breakfast, I watch a doe and a spotted fawn emerge from the woods for a drink. Cautiously, the doe looks around and then dips her muzzle into the water. The fawn plays in the tall grass, occasionally leaps in the air, makes half turns, runs and stops. All of this is ignored by the mother, who alternately drinks and looks and smells, making sure that all is safe for the unknowing youngster who continues to play.

~ Sometimes I believe we need to rethink the meaning of community, of people living near each other in the same place. There are also plant communities, animal communities, pond communities, and upland communities. Human communities are a part of these communities, too. One big community, all living together, all receiving and all giving, all depending on one another for survival.

MA'S BANANA CAKE

2 cups flour
1 1/2 cups sugar
3 teaspoons baking powder
1 teaspoon salt
7 unbeaten egg yolks
3/4 cup cold water
1/2 cup vegetable oil
1 medium ripe banana, mashed
1 teaspoon vanilla
7 egg whites
1/2 teaspoon cream of tartar

Mix the dry ingredients together in a large bowl.

Make a well in dry ingredients. Add yolks, water, and oil. Mix well. Add the banana and vanilla.

Put egg whites and cream of tartar in small bowl.

Beat until very stiff peaks form.

Gently fold the beaten egg whites into the flour-liquid mixture by hand, until the mixture is blended.

Gently pour into an ungreased angel-food cake pan. Using a table knife, cut through cake batter to remove any air bubbles.

Bake at 325 degrees for 55 minutes.

Increase temperature to 350 degrees and bake for 10 more minutes.

Remove from oven and turn pan upside down immediately on a cooling rack. Cool for at least 2 hours.

Remove from pan and serve.

LEAF LETTUCE SALAD

4 to 6 cups leaf lettuce
1/4 cup evaporated milk
1 tablespoon sugar
5 teaspoons vinegar
1/8 teaspoon pepper

Wash and dry lettuce and place in serving bowl.

In a separate small bowl, stir together the milk and sugar. Add vinegar to the milk mixture and stir until mixture thickens.

Add pepper.

Pour mixture over lettuce and serve immediately.

Serves 4 to 6.

August

What About This Weather?

When I was a kid, we did such field work as cultivating corn or plowing with a one-bottom walking plow, and when we came to the end of the field that was the boundary with the neighbor's, we often stopped to rest the horses. When our neighbor was working in his field, he often rested his horses when I did, and we talked across the fence. We talked about the crops and the price of milk (there were all small dairy farms in our community). We talked about the upcoming dance on Saturday night at Lakeside Lodge. And we talked about the weather. We always talked about the weather.

Even today, when guys my age meet, we talk about the weather. It doesn't matter what month it is, what time of day, whether the sun is shining, whether it's pouring down rain or snowing fiercely.

"So what do you think about the weather we're havin'?"

"Sure been a hot one this August."

"Suppose it'll rain today? Sure could use a good rain."

These are the kinds of comments you hear and many more of course, depending on where you live in the country and what season it is.

My wife and I were in Colorado recently, visiting for a few days with my son Jeff, his wife, Sandy, and their three kids, Christian, Nicholas, and Elizabeth. We arrived in a fierce snowstorm that had closed Interstate 70 to all vehicles without chains.

Sixty-mile-an-hour winds blew through downtown Denver, toppling trees and downing power lines. The normally two-hour drive from the airport to Jeff's home took four and a half hours of white-knuckle driving.

This was one of the worst driving experiences I'd had in years. Semitrucks on their sides, car after car in the ditch, a snowplow stuck, red and blue lights flashing everywhere as the snow came down in waves flying on the stiff wind. I wanted to talk about the weather when we arrived at my son's home, tucked high up in the Rockies at 7,500 feet. But no one was talking about the weather.

"People out here don't talk about the weather," our daughter-in-law said.

"Why not?" I asked "There's plenty to talk about."

"They just don't. Mostly they take it as it comes. Weather's not very predictable out here either. Clouds get caught in the mountains, and the weather is mostly a surprise."

In the Midwest, where I come from, we always talked about the weather. Still do.

I was walking not far from my son's home one morning. Snow-covered mountains were all around, and there was some 175 inches of snow in the high country. It was a sight to see as I puffed along, not yet adjusted to the thin air at this altitude. I met a fellow who appeared to be about my age.

"How you doin'?" he asked. "Name is Rich."

"Jerry," I answered, shaking his hand. "Live around here?"

"Yup, right over there," Rich said, pointing. "Where you from?"

"Wisconsin," I answered.

"How's the weather out there?" Rich asked.

So we discussed Midwestern weather for a few minutes as we stood with Rocky Mountains all around us. I was starting to confirm my suspicion that weather was a generational thing, that my son's generation didn't spend time talking about rain or snow and how cold it had gotten the previous night.

Then Rich shared that he had lived in Michigan and that his wife was originally from Ohio. They had moved to Colorado twenty years ago. I was back to the theory that weather is a topic for old guys from the Midwest.

It occurred to me as I pondered this weather thing that those who had grown up on farms might have more interest in the weather than those who grew up in urban areas. Maybe it was being farm born that made the most difference, no matter what part of the country you came from.

When I was a kid, Pa, my two brothers, and I, when the evening chores were done, would stand on the hill back of the barn and watch the sunset. Pa had a way of predicting the following day's weather from the appearance of the sky at sunset and from the wind direction.

Knowing the following day's weather was critical in planning our next day's work. Should we cut down a field of alfalfa? Would we have a few dry days so we could cut the grain field, stand the oat bundles into shocks, and make ready for threshing? A field of shocked oats sitting out in several days of rain and drizzle could spoil the crop. Mold and rot would infest the golden brown grain bundles, the dry oat kernels would germinate, and the hope of saving the crop for winter feed would be lost.

Most times, Pa's weather predictions were correct. We worked our way through summer, always wanting rain, as the crops depended on it, but hoping the rain would not interfere with activities that required dry weather. Never once did I hear Pa curse the rain, for without it we knew we would have no crops.

Watching the sunset was more than weather predicting, though. Pa, my brothers, and I talked about the day's accomplishments—how many loads of hay we'd hauled to the barn, how many acres of potatoes cultivated, or perhaps how many sacks of cucumbers picked. We talked about how the corn was growing and how the cow pastures were surviving the summer—all weather-related conversation.

On those summer days when I woke up with rain pounding on my bedroom window, I would pull on rubber boots, barn coat, and cap and head up the muddy field lane for the cows. Fanny, our collie farm dog, accompanied me as we searched for the herd through the gloomy, dark morning. With the cows found, usually in some secluded hollow, Fanny would walk around each cow and bark a couple times until the cow started toward the barn, dimly seen in the distance. Soon fifteen cows were strung out in a line, one behind the other, slogging along the lane. Fanny walked behind the last cow. I walked behind Fanny, sloshing through the mud and muck.

The cows filed into the barn and took their stalls. Each cow had her own stall, and it never changed, so there was no question of where each cow stood in the barn. With the cows in the barn, Pa and I slammed shut each cow's stanchion, a metal device that confined the cows to their stalls.

Pa had hauled out to the barn two ten-gallon milk cans and our milk pails. Soon we were each under a cow, sitting on three-legged stools with a shiny pail pinched between our legs. Frothy white milk gathered in our milk pails while rainwater dripped from the rain-soaked cows. The smell of fresh milk mixed with that of wet cows, which smell a lot like a wet dog, is not a pleasant experience. I was still wet from walking through the rain, and dripping wet, smelly cows only added to the misery as I sat under them, one after the other.

Pa would say, "Rain before seven, stop before eleven," and he was usually right. With the cows turned back out to pasture in the rain, we hauled the milk cans to the milk house, slipped them into the cooling tank, and went into the house for breakfast. By the time breakfast was finished, the rain had stopped.

"Good day for making fence," Pa said. I loaded cedar fence posts, a posthole digger, an ax, a roll of barbed wire, a hammer, staples, and a shovel on the steel-wheeled wagon before hitching up the team and driving to the cow pasture farthest from the farmstead. The fence separating our farm from the neighbor's was overgrown with oak trees, and dead branches fell on the fence regularly, breaking a wire or sometimes smashing off a post.

Pa hated the late-night phone call from a neighbor: "Herm, your cows are in my corn." Those were words no farmer wanted to hear. The old saying "good fences make for good neighbors" has much truth to it. Fifteen cows in a neighbor's cornfield can cause havoc in an hour. Sometimes a little remedial work— replacing rotting fence posts, tightening a loose wire—prevented the dreaded phone call.

Weather has always been critical to farm life. It dictated what was done and when, and in a larger perspective, it offered up success or failure for most farmers every year.

Farmers, young and old, former and current, definitely still inquire about the weather regularly. But so do lots of other people, especially those who live in the Midwest or once lived there.

August Thoughts

◦ In early August, I rejoice in the first red tomato in my garden, the one I've waited for since last year, the one that signals the start of several weeks of fresh, juicy tomato eating, when the flavor of the garden tomatoes exceeds that of any tomato you buy at the grocery. I carry the tomato into the cabin, slice it open, and sprinkle on a little salt and pepper. I'm not concerned if tomato juice trickles down my chin. After all, I've waited a year for this tasty experience.

◦ Walk a dusty country road that twists and turns and goes uphill and down. It's the mystery of not knowing what is around the next turn and what might lie over the top of the hill that makes these roads so interesting. The mysteries and unknowns add spice to a person's life.

◦ On an early August morning, I watch a big blue heron lift up from the shallows on the west end of the pond when I approach. It flies low over the water and quietly sits down in a shallow bay on the north end. Its early morning feeding has been disturbed but not for long.

◦ A good hen doesn't cackle until she's laid an egg.

~ Some people, when faced with a choice of two roads to take, will take one and halfway along it wish they had taken the other.

~ Every August for a few days, my son and I pitch a tent on the shores of a northern lake, where the only sounds are those of the loon and the gull and the wind rustling through the boughs of pine trees and maples. At night, we sit by a small campfire and watch the flames, the only light in a black night except for the stars. As I sit by the fire, I think about those who traveled here before me for hundreds of years—native people, trappers, and explorers—sitting by similar campfires and reflecting on the day and planning the morrow. Or maybe they just enjoyed the fire that flickered and sputtered and sparked without thinking about anything except how good it was to be alive in this place. I go to bed to the sound of waves teasing the rocks below our campsite and to the sight of a sky so full of stars it seems there should not be room for them all.

~ In August, I eat new potatoes, freshly picked green beans, sliced cucumbers, and cabbage slaw made from the green and plump head I cut an hour earlier. No matter how well food is preserved or processed, nothing tastes better than garden freshness.

~ I have a pile of field stones on the edge of one of my fields. The last great glacier stopped here some ten thousand years ago and brought these rocks with it: red ones, gray ones, striped ones, black jagged ones, some as large as a kitchen stove, many mere pebbles. Some are from as far away as northern Canada. The stones all came with the huge ice sheets that stopped here and melted, left as reminders of the great power of ice.

‿ With my grandsons, I hike my restored prairie and notice the big bluestem grass now five and more feet tall; milkweed in full flower with monarch butterfly visitors; early goldenrod, a striking yellow; the pale pinkish green leaves of the dotted mint; and the purple spikes of the blazing star that are just beginning to open. These are my payment for the patience and the little work it's taking to restore to prairie what was once a cornfield.

‿ Sometimes it takes awhile to realize that we can't know everything.

‿ I hike along a trail on a dark night. A stiff wind blows from the west, cooling the parched, dry land. I hear a sound—an eerie, almost guttural noise, a sound I haven't heard before. My imagination soars. Has some new animal or bird moved onto my land from parts unknown? Or is a known creature making an unknown sound? I shine the flashlight beam among the tree branches, the location of the sound. And I spot the source. Two dead tree branches are rubbing together as the breeze rustles the treetops. My imagination is disappointed.

‿ Dry and hot weather has browned the grass and turned some of the trees to premature fall colors. Thunderclouds have boiled in the west all afternoon. After the sun goes down, the western sky fills with flashes of lightning. Soon thunder shakes the parched earth and a sharp wind moves the trees. A few drops of rain hit the cabin's stone step and immediately evaporate. And the storm moves on east. The drought is far from broken. How hard it is for rain to fall when it is so badly needed.

‿ Be careful of the past; it always looks better than it was.

◡ I take a bushel basket to the garden and fill it with ripe and nearly ripe tomatoes. Hot, dry weather has favored the tomato crop. The fruit is round and firm and without blemish. Soon Ruth has a huge kettle of tomatoes cooking on the kitchen stove, and by late afternoon, jars of homemade tomato soup line up on the counter. The smell of cooking tomatoes remains in the kitchen—a wonderfully rich smell that sends gardeners back to their youth, and to their mothers' kettles of cooking tomatoes.

◡ In the near dark of early evening, I spot a brown bird sitting on the ground alongside the trail. As I approach, it doesn't move. It's a woodcock—a bird I haven't seen for years. The woodcock is easy to identify because of its long bill, big head, and eyes that are large and set back. The woodcock nests on the ground, so the dry weather must have helped it. Later in the fall, the bird, when approached, will rise straight up on its short wings, making a whistling sound and pleasing even the most uninterested observer.

◡ Table salt becomes damp before rain.

◡ Ruth and I stand on a hillside covered with wildflowers—a palette of yellows, golds, purples, and blues. We enjoy their beauty, how the colors contrast with each other, with the green grass, with the dull green of pine trees in the distance, with the blue sky. I don't worry about naming each flower today. Sometimes naming can get in the way of enjoying.

◡ I watch a red-tailed hawk sitting high in a poplar tree, nearly motionless. Then it screeches its eerie call, and I wonder why it has announced its presence. An old-timer told me once that when the hawk calls, the field mice that are hiding in the grass hear it and try to scamper for cover. Their movement reveals their location, and the keen-eyed hawk swoops down from the tree for lunch—another example of what seems a contradiction in nature being in reality a clever ruse.

～ Watch the new moon. If it's tipped so you can't hang a pail of water on its tip, rain is coming.

～ The higher the clouds, the better the weather.

～ Four-letter words to think about:
  Give
  Sing
  Feel
  Look
  Grin
  Hear

～ I notice the woodbine vine crawling up several trees. Its five-leaf clusters, sometimes confused with the itchy three-leafed poison ivy, are beginning to turn a brilliant red. First signs of fall. A harbinger of seasonal change.

HOMEMADE TOMATO SOUP

6 onions, chopped
1 bunch celery, chopped
6 quarts tomatoes, coarsely chopped, stems and spots
removed (use 3 quarts for very thick mixture)
1 cup sugar
4 tablespoons lemon juice
2 tablespoons salt
1 cup butter or margarine
1 cup flour

Begin cooking onions and celery in a large kettle, adding a little water to prevent sticking. Add tomatoes to the pan and cook at a medium temperature until all are soft.

Push through a sieve. Put tomato pulp back in kettle and begin heating. Add sugar, lemon juice, and salt to tomato pulp.

Combine butter or margarine and flour in a small bowl.

Add a small amount, about a cup, of the soup mixture to the flour mixture until blended. Add flour mixture to simmering soup, stirring constantly until the soup is thickened to the consistency of gravy. Bring to a boil.

Pour into hot, sterilized pint jars. Seal and process in boiling hot water bath for 15 minutes.

Remove and cool. Store and enjoy.

If tomatoes are juicy, makes around 13 pints.

CREAMY CUCUMBERS

1/2 cup vinegar
1/2 cup cold water
1 teaspoon salt
5 peppercorns
1 medium cucumber (about 8 inches long)
1/4 to 1/3 cup sour cream

Put vinegar, water, and salt into a bowl and mix together.

Peel, score, and slice cucumber. Add cucumber slices to vinegar-water mixture. Chill for at least 2 hours.

Drain. Add sour cream.

Coat cucumbers and serve immediately.

September

School Days

The beginning of September brings back memories of the one-room country school I attended for eight years. Today the old schoolhouse, in the town of Rose, Waushara County, Wisconsin, is a family home. Outwardly it appears as it did in the late 1930s and 1940s, when I was a student there.

By today's standards, the school was primitive. The building, of wooden construction, was about forty feet long and half as wide. It faced east and had tall windows on both the south and north sides. The windows provided the light we needed for studying, as the school had no electricity until the early 1940s. A bell tower, containing a big cast-iron bell that could be heard for miles, was perched on the roof of the school, near the front. Inside, the furnishings were sparse. A wood-burning stove provided the necessary heat; when the outside temperatures dropped below zero, the stove tried to make the room comfortable, but never quite succeeded. On the coldest days, we all sat near the stove to keep warm. A Red Wing stoneware water cooler sat next to the sink. A student filled the cooler each morning with water pumped by hand from a well in the nearby combination pump house and woodshed.

A big, brown upright piano stood next to the teacher's desk at the front of the room. On the other side of the teacher's desk was a sandbox on legs, where we created nature displays we learned about from listening to *Afield with Ranger Mac,* a weekly radio program broadcast from the University of Wisconsin in Madison. Ranger Mac was really Wakelin McNeil, a professor in the College of Agriculture and also the state 4-H club leader. A battery-powered Philco radio sat on one corner of the teacher's desk. Only the teacher was allowed to turn on the radio, since the school board, frugal in every respect, purchased but one battery a year. Ranger Mac spoke about everything from how snowflakes develop to how lake ice forms to the inner workings of an anthill. Farm kids lived in nature. We did farm chores, walked to school, and were outside most of the time. Yet each of us was fascinated with Ranger Mac's programs and his activities, which we could try in our sandbox, an important part of our nature corner. We were not alone. Several thousand one-room school pupils throughout Wisconsin and beyond listened to this Peabody Award–winning radio program and built nature corners in their schools. I credit Ranger Mac for instilling in me an interest in biology, forestry, and nature study, and a love for the land that continues to this day.

I remember my teachers well. At the time, I didn't realize how difficult it was to teach in a one-room country school. These teachers had so many responsibilities it's a wonder that most succeeded. For example, the teacher arrived at least an hour before school started each morning, and even earlier in winter when she had to start the fire in the woodstove. (The vast majority of the teachers were young women, some of them still in their teens.) On below-zero mornings, the inside of the schoolroom was as cold as an icehouse freshly packed with ice.

One-room-school teachers taught all eight grades. Our school had no kindergarten, so kids went immediately into first grade as early as age five. The better teachers soon learned the strengths and weaknesses of each student. They combined student classes based on ability rather than grade. For instance, if you were good at reading and in third grade, you might meet with the fifth-grade reading class. If you were in third grade and having problems with math, the teacher might ask a seventh- or eighth-grade student to work with you.

One-room-school teachers were great psychologists and assigned duties for each student to perform. Duties ranged from cleaning the blackboard erasers (a duty for a first grader), carrying in wood and water, washing the blackboards, sweeping out the boys' and girls' outhouses, and putting up and taking down the American flag from its outdoor flagpole at the beginning and end of the school day.

Duties were generally not seen as punishment for wrongdoing but as expected jobs for everyone. The teacher wanted students to look forward to what she called higher-level duties, those usually performed by seventh- and eighth-grade students. From year to year, most students tried to perform their duties as well as possible, without being told, and always on time. If you were a seventh grader and your duty was to keep the woodstove filled with wood all day, you didn't wait for the teacher to remind you to go for more wood. Likewise, if you were in eighth grade and responsible for keeping the water cooler filled, you kept an eye on it and went out to the pump house and pumped more water when necessary. At day's end, especially in winter, you knew to dump the remaining water from the water cooler so it wouldn't freeze overnight.

The most prestigious duty was putting up and taking down the flag. This duty was usually reserved for an eighth grader who had a seven-year exemplary record for performing duties.

Duties were not a written part of the school curriculum, but many important skills, values, and attitudes were learned doing them. These values included doing a task without being told; doing every task, no matter how menial, to the best of your ability; trying always to do more than expected; and not seeking or receiving praise for a job well done. These lessons, taught through doing, remain forever with most former country-school kids.

Of course, there were always one or two students who shirked on their duties and didn't move on to those deemed more lofty and prestigious. One of my schoolmate's duties was to sweep the boys' toilet every day for two years. I don't recall what duty violation he committed, but the teacher knew and took appropriate action. The teacher always knew.

Besides supervising all the duties that school kids performed and teaching all eight grades, a country-school teacher was also the school nurse, social worker, physical education teacher, music teacher, art teacher, and janitor. She of course also had to follow all the many county and state rules and regulations.

I recall one day when I was in seventh grade, and our teacher, Maxine Thompson, returned from the school mailbox with a package that was about the size of two loaves of homemade bread.

"Wonder what this is?" she said as she searched for some scissors to cut the string wrapped around the bundle. It was recess, and several of us gathered around the teacher's desk as she unwrapped it.

"It's from Madison," she said, frowning. Correspondence from Madison, meaning the State Superintendent of Schools office, usually meant extra work for the teacher.

"Safety patrol equipment," she said as she pulled out several white canvas belts with badges attached. The belts were popularly called Sam Brownie belts, and they were the kind that went over your shoulder and fastened around your waist. There were seven belts and badges total, and the colors of the badges denoted various safety patrol positions: blue was for the captain, red was for the two lieutenants, black was for the four patrol officers. Miss Thompson read the accompanying letter.

"We must organize a safety patrol," she said, putting down the letter. "It is to protect all the children from traffic as they arrive at and go home from school." She said this with a straight face. We kids looked at each other in wonderment. The only traffic by our school was the mailman, who came about eleven each day; the milkman, who picked up milk from area farms and drove by about ten; Floyd Jeffers, who drove by perhaps once a week on his way to town for groceries; and Weston Coombes, who came by every couple weeks driving his horse hitched to a buggy because the Coombes family didn't own a car. That was the extent of the traffic past our school—so few vehicles that if we happened to be outside for recess or noon break and a car passed, we ran to the school fence to see who it was. I don't recall that there was ever any traffic in the morning when we arrived at school, nor in the afternoon when school let out.

Nonetheless, Miss Thompson, following the state's mandate, organized a school safety patrol. Bob Zubeck, in eighth grade, became captain. I was in seventh grade, so I became a lieutenant; the other lieutenant position remained vacant. Jim Kolka, Mildred Swendryznski, Jerry Zubeck, and Dave Kolka became patrol officers. They took turns standing duty from 8:30 to 9 each morning and 4 to 4:15 each afternoon. My job as lieutenant was to make sure the patrol officers were at their assigned stations each morning and afternoon.

The weeks went by. The novelty of being a patrol officer with a fancy white canvas belt and badge began to wear off. It was mighty boring standing alongside the dusty dirt road as children marched through the school gate each morning and afternoon with nary a car or buggy in sight.

Every four weeks, Miss Thompson submitted a report to Madison on patrol activities—how many children were saved from automobiles, how many near-misses there were, that sort of thing. At the end of the fall term, a big envelope arrived in our school mailbox. It was a certificate of commendation for our safety patrol and its exemplary record of protecting children as they arrived and left school. Miss Thompson hadn't reported—the report forms didn't ask—that only a handful of cars, trucks, and horse-drawn buggies had driven by the school all fall and almost none were observed during the time the children were arriving and leaving school.

Sometime during the spring term yet another letter arrived from Madison. It stated that isolated rural schools, such as ours, were no longer required to "mount school safety patrols." Miss Thompson collected the safety patrol belts and badges, put them in a box, and stored the collection alongside the stove in the back of the room. Years later, on rainy days, children looking for games to play at noon break would come upon the box of belts and badges, finger them, and wonder what they were.

September Thoughts

~ Some people never let grass grow under their feet because they never move out of their tracks.

~ A fellow, when asked if he expected to loaf all the time, replied, "Nope, I've got to find some time to sleep."

~ On a cloudy, early evening, I hear an owl call from deep in the woods, and a few seconds later another owl answers. The sound echoes through the valley and resembles a person saying, "Who cooks for you; who cooks for you?" And, as if challenging the owl calls, a wild turkey gobbles. This continues: owl calls, turkey gobbles. It's a strange plethora of wild sound, filling the valley to the west of the cabin and echoing up the hill.

~ When you whack a hornet's nest, expect to be stung.

~ In early September, the garden continues to produce, especially zucchini squash. We search for new ways of enjoying it, realizing every year that we've planted too many hills. Fortunately, zucchini bread has become a favorite of our children and grandchildren.

~ Here in the north, the best wood for fence posts, in order of their durability, are black locust, red cedar, and white cedar.

The worst is white pine. The oaks (red, white, bur, and black) are somewhere in between.

∼ We are all tied to the natural world, to the changing of the seasons, to the darkness of night and the brightness of day, to the tiny blue asters that struggle on a sandy hillside, to the bald eagle that soars overhead. Remember to:

Watch the sunset.

Enjoy a cool glass of well water.

Find humor when nothing seems funny.

Do something extra for the special person in your life.

Walk in the rain.

Occasionally do nothing—and enjoy it.

∼ When I come upon an old barn in my travels, I often stop. I look at its shape and size. I see the craftsmanship in the masonry walls and the beauty of the barn boards. I think about the stories the old barn holds—stories of family farmers making a living on the land and focusing their attention on the barn, for here is where their cattle, the main source of their income, was housed. Here is where they spent several hours of the day, 365 days of the year.

∼ As I stand under a big bur oak tree, I touch the gnarled and rugged bark and look at the huge sturdy branches. The width of the tree's branches is nearly as great as its height. The tree may be one hundred years old, two hundred years, or even older. This tree was here when the first settlers came to the Midwest in the early 1800s. It is a living piece of history, standing tall and impressive in the present.

~ I show the grandkids a hornet's nest, tucked under the roof of the pump house. We keep a goodly distance away so as not to bother the hornets as they work to gather food. I help the grandkids both respect and understand that hornets have a place in the world, too.

~ In any journey, it's important to stop from time to time and be thankful for the distance you've covered.

~ After a recent rain and several warm days, the goldenrods show full color—yellow counterpoints to a field of otherwise brown, dry grass.

~ It's important to know who you are even when there is no one else around.

~ With the grandchildren, I watch an anthill, the scurry of activity of ants that are working hard, doing what they are supposed to be doing. No ant is standing around, watching, wondering, waiting. No ant appears to be complaining or worried that its work has gone unrecognized. All contribute to a common goal, cooperating and sharing.

~ On a rainy day in September, I recall an old mariner's proverb: "Some rain, some rest; fine weather isn't always best."

~ My prairie is studded with blazing star showing the promise of a wonderful purple display, but I see the results of drought: dried stems; crisp, never opened flowers. Great promise destroyed by the weather. Next year?

~ After weeks of brutally dry weather, I wake up in the night to the sound of the wind blowing and rain striking the cabin windows. I open a window and smell the rich aroma of dry, thirsty grass getting a drink of water.

～ In the white pine woodlot south of the cabin, I pick up a pinecone and look at it carefully. The seeds, each one tucked under its own woody scale, are tiny and frail, and have transparent wings that fly on the wind and spread the seeds over great distances. The scales—arranged in a symmetrical form, each layered over the one beneath it, like shingles on a roof—protect each other and yet stay out of each other's way. I count the scales, some sixty of them, a potential for sixty seeds and sixty trees. But only a few seeds will find a fertile place, and even fewer trees will survive their first years, when deer especially relish the new growth.

～ A few years ago, I learned that I have several "invasive" plants on my farm. This means I have plants that are not native to the area. These unwanted plants include buckthorn, box elder, black locust, and honeysuckle. They grow fast, and they crowd out the native plants. From a forester I hear about alternative ways of ridding my farm of these competitive rascals. When the professional spiel is over, I realize how difficult the task will be.

～ Frost hangs on the grass and crunches underfoot this morning. I spot a tiny cobweb, no more than a couple inches across. Ordinarily invisible, it has been turned white by the frost, and it sparkles in the first rays of the morning sun. It is like a tiny painting in a great art museum that is sometimes overlooked because of all that surrounds it. This dainty little cobweb has its moment of glory on this frosty, sunny morning.

～ I listen to a small flock of Canada geese as they wing low over the trees around the pond. Locals probably, out searching for their morning breakfast. It is still too early for the migrants from the north to pass through on their way to their winter homes.

⟿ Morning frost covers the grass in the field to the south of the cabin, and frost appears on the cabin roof as well. It's the first frost of the season and a sign that autumn is fast approaching.

⟿ On the day of my eighth-grade teacher's funeral, I recall how she helped whet my interest in nature and the outdoors. I remember the field trips we took around the lake that was just down the hill from the country school. I remember the discussions she led after we listened to Ranger Mac's nature program on the state radio station. I applaud her today, for she never once said that a question was dumb or inappropriate. "Never quit asking questions," she more than once said. "It's how we all learn."

⟿ It's time to dig the rutabagas that grow on the north end of the garden. I've mostly forgotten the beggies, as we call them, because I've been harvesting tomatoes, cucumbers, green peppers, carrots, cabbage, green beans, onions, and beets the past several weeks. Now I pull the rutabagas and lay them out to dry before I top them and toss them into a basket. An average crop, maybe below average because the late-July and August rains were absent this season. Some are plump and well formed; others are stunted and I leave them behind. Good seasons and less good seasons, like life itself.

ZUCCHINI BREAD

3 eggs
1 cup vegetable oil
2 cups sugar
2 cups zucchini, grated and peeled
2 teaspoons vanilla
3 cups flour
1 teaspoon soda
1/2 teaspoon baking powder
1 teaspoon salt
1 teaspoon ground cinnamon

Preheat oven to 325 degrees. Grease and flour 3 pans (7 1/2 x 3 3/4 x 2 1/4 -inch).

In a bowl, beat eggs. Add oil, sugar, zucchini, and vanilla. Mix together well.

Sift and mix dry ingredients together.

Add dry ingredients to egg mixture and mix until thoroughly blended. Divide mixture among the pans.

Bake 45 to 50 minutes, until bread is brown and pulls away from sides of pan.

Note: You can double the recipe if you have a large bowl for mixing the egg mixture and the flour mixture. Make sure that flour is well mixed with the other ingredients. The expanded recipe makes 6 to 7 loaves.

COOKED RUTABAGAS

1 medium rutabaga (about 1 1/2 pounds)
1 tablespoon butter
2 teaspoons honey

Wash and peel rutabaga. Cut into small cubes and cook in boiling water until soft, about 25 to 30 minutes. Drain. Put in serving bowl.

Serve plain or drizzle with melted butter.

For added flavor, melt butter and honey together. Mix with hot rutabaga and serve.

Serves 4.

October

Potato Vacation

In early October, when the leaves were turning color and the Canada geese had begun winging south, our country school closed for two weeks. It was called "potato vacation," but it wasn't much of a vacation at all. True, school wasn't in session. But all the community children, rather than sitting in school each morning, gathered in their parents' potato fields to help with the potato harvest. Some vacation. It was mostly hard and often cold work.

A little background. During pioneer days, starting in the 1850s and continuing well into the 1870s, wheat was the main agricultural crop in much of our part of the Midwest. By the early 1880s, when wheat was no longer profitable, farmers searched for other ways to make a living. Cash crops became popular—hops in parts of southern Wisconsin; canning crops in eastern counties; tobacco in Vernon, Dane, Rock, and a few other counties; and potatoes in central Wisconsin. Potatoes prefer sandy, acidic soil, and that's what we had in our part of the state. By 1900, dairy farming had become the predominant source of farm income, but many farmers clung to the cash crops they had come to depend on for a part of their farm income.

During the 1940s, potatoes were an especially profitable crop, so nearly every farmer in our community grew at least ten acres, some twenty acres, of potatoes. By today's standards, what we were doing doesn't sound like much. (Today, potato growers may plant and harvest a thousand acres of potatoes.) But there were no tractors, no fancy machines of any kind to help with the work. The potatoes were planted by hand. A farmer used a potato planter, a handheld implement that he stuck in the ground and dropped a potato seed into. Then he pushed the planter forward, pulled it out, and dragged his foot across the hole to cover the seed. He carried a sack of potato seeds slung over his shoulder. As he walked, you could hear the methodical *clup clup* of the potato planter closing, following the mark in the ground earlier made by a wooden marker pulled by a horse. Planting potatoes was backbreaking work, especially when the potato rows were eighty rods long and the land was hilly.

Potatoes required attention all summer long—not like alfalfa that once planted is left to grow. Potatoes had to be cultivated. One of my early jobs was walking behind a one-horse-drawn cultivator, holding the handles and trying to steer a path down the center of the row without burying or, worse, cutting out a potato plant. Once the potatoes were cultivated, which had to be done several times until the plants were tall enough to shade the rows, we hoed around the plants to remove any weeds that the cultivator had not destroyed. Hour after hour we hoed, up the hills and down the hills and through the valleys that were often infested with quack grass, which was nearly impossible to remove.

When there were no other jobs to do on the farm, we knew the potatoes needed hoeing. The potatoes always needed hoeing, just like the fences always needed fixing. These were the never-ending jobs. If the rains came regularly that year, the potato crop was a good one. If there were dry periods during the summer, the potatoes suffered along with the corn, oats, alfalfa, and pasture crops. But the potatoes suffered more, because potatoes require lots of water to grow well. (Today, almost all the potatoes in central Wisconsin are grown on irrigated land, where the crop receives the amount of water it needs.)

In October, the first frosts, which killed the potato vines, signaled the first day of potato harvesting season (and potato vacation). Pa and the hired man found six-tine forks and headed to the potato field. Pa drove the team hitched to the steel-wheeled wagon, which was piled high with wooden bushel-size potato crates. My brothers and I sat on the side of the wagon, our legs hanging off. We each had a five-gallon pail—they had been paint pails that Pa had gotten somewhere. He had burned the paint out of them and washed them.

Once out in the potato field, Pa drove the length of the field, distributing potato boxes every few yards along the way. Then he tied the team to the fence, under an oak tree, and he and the hired man began digging. Each man dug two rows at a time. They backed down the field between the rows, digging the fresh, earth-smelling potatoes, shaking off the vines and allowing the potatoes to gather on the soft, sandy soil between the rows. I grabbed my pail and began picking potatoes behind Pa. Darrel and Donald picked behind the hired man. *Bang, bang, bang* was the sound as the potatoes struck the bottom of the pail. Soon the sound was a dull thud as potatoes struck other potatoes. When my pail was full, I carried it to one of the wooden boxes, dumped it, and returned to picking. Potato after potato, pail after pail, bushel box after bushel box. We had one great incentive for our work: Pa paid us a penny for every bushel of potatoes we picked, and if the potatoes were good, we could each pick one hundred bushels in a day and earn one dollar.

Pa and the hired man carried on a conversation as they worked. I thought about how I would spend all the money I was earning and how good it was to be out of school for two weeks. About halfway through the morning, about all I could think about was how hungry I was. I didn't have a watch, so I glanced regularly at the sun moving across the autumn sky to tell me when it was noon. I usually figured it was twelve o'clock about an hour before it actually was; one's hunger often influences what one sees.

About a half hour or so before noon, Pa said it was time to load up. I fetched the team from where they had spent the morning lazing under the big oak tree, and we drove the length of the field, picking up filled potato boxes and stacking them on the wagon. By the time the wagon was loaded, it was piled several boxes high. Pa tied a rope around the boxes to keep them from tipping off the wagon, and we headed home, my brothers and I and the hired man sitting on the top of the boxes while Pa drove the team.

We stored the potatoes in one of two places: the cellar under the house, which had a dirt floor and was divided with boards into potato bins, or the potato cellar that stood just west of the chicken house and was dug partially underground, as it backed up to a rather steep hill.

To dump the potatoes into the bins under the house, Pa drove the team next to an outside door that opened to some steep steps leading to the cellar. He had placed a two-by-ten-inch wooden plank alongside the steps. The hired man grabbed a potato box off the wagon and slid it down the steep plank, where Pa caught it on the bottom and dumped the potatoes into the bin. My job was to pull the bushel crates to the edge of the wagon, where the hired man could easily grab them. We dumped box after box of potatoes until the wagon was empty.

Pa drove the team to the water tank for a drink and then to the barn where he gave them some oats. With our noon meal finished, it was back out to the potato field—day after day, bushel after bushel, until I didn't want to see or smell another potato. The two October weeks of potato vacation sped by. Some mornings, white frost covered the ground, and I shivered my way across the field until the sun came up, melted the frost, and warmed me.

A day or two before potato vacation was over, we usually finished harvesting our crop. The bins under the house were full;

the bins in the potato cellar were filled as well. With some potato vacation remaining, Pa sometimes helped out the neighbors with their crop, and he volunteered us to help with the picking. Alan Davis couldn't afford a hired man, so he welcomed our help. The only good thing about working at the neighbors' was knowing that it would last only a day or two and potato vacation would end and we'd all be back in school, catching up on our lessons, and thinking about what we would buy with the money we earned.

Taking care of the potatoes didn't end with the harvesting. We had to sell them. The market was usually poor at harvest time, much better in mid-winter. So as soon as below-freezing temperatures arrived, we began keeping a stove going in the potato cellar. One more chore. We now had four stoves to keep stocked with wood. In addition to the big rusty beast in the potato cellar, we had a stove in the pump house, a cookstove in the kitchen, and another wood burner in the dining room.

On a warm day in January, when the temperature climbed above freezing, Pa would announce one day at breakfast, "It's time to sack up them spuds in the potato cellar."

When the chores were done at night, Pa and I would spend a couple hours, by the light of a kerosene lantern, forking potatoes onto a hand-cranked potato sorter that allowed the little potatoes to drop through and the larger ones to move along until they tumbled into a big burlap potato sack fastened to the end of the contraption. We dragged the filled potato sack onto a platform scale, making sure that each sack contained a hundred pounds, sometimes a little more because Pa never wanted to cheat anybody. Pa then sewed each sack shut with a huge needle and binding twine. When he was finished, the filled potato sack had two ears and a neat row of sewing across the top. The ears provided convenient handles for lifting the heavy sacks.

The next day, Pa would load the potato sacks on a bobsled pulled by our team and drive the four miles to Wild Rose, where the potato warehouses were lined up along the Chicago and Northwestern railroad tracks. On the front end of the sleigh was a little shelter—a sleigh coupe, it was called. The little wooden building, about four feet square, had a metal roof. It had a board seat inside for two people, who could see out the big window facing the team. Under the window was a slot where the driving lines from the horses would slide. A small metal stove on legs stood in the corner of the little building. Riding to town in winter, with the stove going and a stream of smoke pouring from its little stove pipe that stuck out the roof, was not an unpleasant event.

Pa filled the bottom of the sleigh with fresh straw and covered the filled potato sacks with horse blankets so the potatoes wouldn't chill. Arriving in Wild Rose, he would dicker a little with the dealers, sell his load, and head back home. If the weather stayed relatively mild, he kept hauling potatoes until the potato cellar was empty. We all looked forward to that day, for now there was one less chore to do—keeping the potato cellar stove going.

Potatoes took up much of our time on the farm when I was a kid, but they brought in some much needed additional money to pay taxes and other farm expenses. My brothers and I both dreaded and looked forward to the annual potato vacation at our school—a vacation, I learned years later, that was unique to country school kids and not known by kids living in other parts of the Midwest.

October Thoughts

❧ Hard frost is predicted this October evening, so I grab the six-tine fork and head for the potato patch in my garden. Soon freshly dug potatoes are spread out before me as I back my way between two rows, digging first to my left, then to my right. Every hill I dig is a surprise—four potatoes, five potatoes, a huge potato, a potato shaped like a rabbit. As I dig, my mind is filled with potato delicacies: baked potatoes, cottage fries, boiled potatoes, potato soup, escalloped potatoes and ham, fried potatoes and eggs, potato pancakes. And the digging is easier and the pain in my back lessens.

❧ When the horse dies, it's time to climb off.

❧ I enjoy the smell of wood smoke trickling from the kitchen stove when I return from a hike on a crisp, frosty morning. I think about when I was a kid and how the smell of wood smoke meant not only warmth, but also family, hearty meals, and good stories.

❧ You can count the number of seeds in an apple, but the number of apples in a seed will remain forever a mystery.

❧ As in cards, we must play the hand dealt us in life. Winning isn't as important as playing a poor hand well.

∾ Looking at nature is not the same as living with it.

∾ As a cold October sun slowly peeks above the horizon, I walk
the trail south of the house and spot a ruffed grouse, its neck
feathers puffed in colorful display. Then grouse explode from
the underbrush—one, two, three—and I lose count because
several fly up together. They evoke memories of an earlier
day, when I carried a shotgun in search of this elusive bird,
but was usually so surprised when they burst up in front of
me that I didn't even raise the gun to my shoulder.

∾ Buckthorn it is called—a not-unattractive shrub with shiny
green leaves and black berries that hang heavy in the fall. But
it is despised by the professional foresters. Not native. An
invasive species, they say with disdain. Must be removed so
more favorable plants can grow. Many of the people living in
these parts were not native, but immigrants, invasive species.

∾ The storm comes up quickly, booming out of the southwest
with thunder and lightning and drenching rain. I pull up
the hood on my parka and stand under a big pine tree, one
smaller than those around it, for I know the ways of lightning. Soon raindrops are dripping from the pine needles, and
the smell of fresh pine is everywhere—a smell that so many
have tried to duplicate but none have succeeded in doing.

∾ Watch out for deer when you drive in the country. October
is the start of the rut, that time of the year when bucks and
does seek to add numbers to the species. Driving at dusk
is especially precarious, as hormone-driven deer jump in
front of your car and race this way and that with no concern
for roads and automobiles. The rut is an eons-old biolog-
ical event—only in recent years have autos made it more
precarious.

~ Take time to "read" a block of wood before you swing the splitting maul. Take time to "read" a person before you open your mouth.

~ It is an unfortunate person who does not have wood to split, a garden to hoe, or a trail to hike.

~ Take your family to a "pick yourself" orchard. With the apples, make applesauce. It's not that difficult, and eating homemade applesauce with homemade bread during the cold days of winter can be very special.

~ Good things can be accomplished in many ways.

~ A cold rain beats on the bedroom window when I wake up. It brings back memories of my growing-up years on the farm— walking to school along the country road as rain dripped from the trees and shrubs, my wool coat getting soaked through by the time I arrived at the schoolhouse.

~ On an early morning hike, the morning sun rises above the white pines to the east, lighting the tops of the brilliant yellow birch trees while their chalky white trunks remain in the shadows. Nothing this early morning is as beautiful. It is as if Mother Nature chose to feature birch leaves today, putting the spotlight full on them. Tomorrow morning it might be a maple or an oak or maybe a white pine. But this day it is birch leaves that are receiving attention.

~ At my pond on a frosty morning, a few fingers of mist lift from the water. The pond and the land around it are waiting; within a month, the pond will freeze, and the trees that surround it will stand naked until April, when the seasonal cycle will repeat. Now, the land is preparing for a long rest after the seasons of birth, growth, and harvest.

∼ How you swing the ax isn't nearly as important as where the ax blade strikes the tree.

∼ Learn from many; be taught by all.

∼ The radio blares the weather report: "Cloudy, brisk northwest wind, snow squalls in the north, maybe some accumulation." I am still hoping for a long pleasant autumn, in spite of the forecast. Sometimes hope and reality clash—usually go with hope.

∼ I look for cattails in a marshy area near a pond. I enjoy the brown cigars perched on long sturdy stems. The cigars are really brown flower clusters, and as cold weather arrives, they begin coming apart, scattering seeds on the wind.

∼ A gentle, drizzly rain starts in the early evening and continues through the night, sending once-brilliant red and yellow maple leaves drifting to the ground, where they accumulate in soggy masses. The shift is occurring, from early fall with its spender of color—reds, yellows, browns—to bare branches that stand naked in the rain. The celebration of the season is ending and hints of a long winter are emerging.

∼ Fog sneaks in during the night, quietly, without fuss. In the morning, I can see only dimly the pump house, and it is less than a hundred yards away. The back shed is lost from sight completely. I walk the woods trail feeling very alone. It is like walking inside a closet that moves as I move. It is at the same time eerie and comforting.

∼ If you put all your eggs in one basket, be sure to keep your eye on that basket.

~ Several tamarack trees grow alongside a little field south of my cabin. The tamarack is a living contradiction. It appears to be a conifer, like the pines, spruces, and firs. But with the first hard frost, its delicate, light green needles turn a golden yellow, as yellow as the aspens that grow on the hills nearby. The tamarack, unlike other needle-leaved trees, drops its needles in the fall, starting over again with new ones the following spring, following the way of the deciduous trees such as the oaks and maples. Native people have used the tamarack for food and medicine and have used the roots to make woven baskets. Pioneers used the tree for everything from house and barn frames to fence posts; the wood is sturdy and extremely weather resistant. The tamarack is a tree with a long history and that continues to delight today.

RUTH'S APPLESAUCE

3 to 4 pounds of cooking apples
Water
1 cup sugar
3/4 teaspoon cinnamon

Wash apples. Cut into quarters and place in a big kettle with a small amount of water. Stir to prevent sticking. Bring to a boil and then simmer until the apples are soft. Stir occasionally.

Put apples through a food mill to remove peels and seeds from the pulp.

Measure out 4 cups apple pulp. Put the pulp in the kettle. Add sugar and cinnamon.

Bring to boil, stirring constantly. Reduce heat and simmer for 4 to 5 minutes.

Put applesauce in clean, sterilized pint jars, leaving 1/2 inch head space. Wipe lip of jar. Seal with two-piece caps.

Process jars 20 minutes in boiling water bath. Remove from canner. Let cool away from drafts.

Store in a cool, dark cupboard.

November

Preparations for Winter

Life on the farm in the Midwest is a cycle of seasonal work: soil preparation and planting in spring, weeding in summer, harvesting in late summer and early fall, preparation for winter, and the long days of winter work.

When the harvesting was finished in the fall; the silo filled with chopped corn; the remaining corn cut, shocked, husked, and forked into the corncribs; and the potatoes dug and stored in the potato cellar, work turned to preparation for winter.

Farm life in the north revolves around winter. When I was a kid on the farm, as soon as the last cob of corn was forked into the corncrib, "making wood" became a priority. Farm folks have their own language; they often use words and phrases that cause city people to respond, "Huh? What did you say?" There is no such thing as making wood in a literal sense. But every farmer knows that "making wood" means cutting and splitting a huge pile of wood to keep hungry woodstoves satisfied during the usually cold and often long winter.

Making wood was only one of several tasks required to prepare for winter. We also banked the foundation of our farmhouse. To do this, we unrolled tarpaper and wrapped it around the entire foundation. Once the tarpaper was in place, Pa hitched the team to the hay wagon, piled the wagon high with straw, and then drove to the house, where we packed straw all around the house's foundation. We left it there until April, depending on when the winter snows melted and the first warm temperatures returned.

The tarpaper and straw kept the frigid winds of winter from seeping into the house. Some of our neighbors went one step further to bank their houses: they piled cow and horse manure all around the foundations. Aside from the smell, which was minimal during the cold days of winter, the manure created some of its own heat as it decomposed, making it doubly effective. The disadvantage of using manure as banking material usually was revealed in the spring, when the temperature began rising, the manure thawed, and strong barnyard smells wafted into the house. My mother never allowed Pa to pile manure around our house, no matter how effective it was when the northwest winds rattled the windows on a below-zero day.

November also meant Armistice Day (November 11), when all the kids at our country school stood facing east for a couple of minutes at eleven o'clock. We were, of course, remembering the end of World War I, when on the eleventh hour of the eleventh day of the eleventh month in 1918, the "war to end all wars" came to a halt.

At the country school in November, we studied the Pilgrims' first Thanksgiving, making cutouts and pictures of pilgrims, turkeys, squash, corn, and pumpkins and using them to decorate the schoolroom. We discussed what it must have been like at that first Thanksgiving, when the Indians and the Pilgrims celebrated together.

Of course, we also celebrated our own Thanksgiving. Ma usually invited my Aunt Louise, whose husband had died several years earlier, and my Aunt Arvilla and her two boys, Ron and Bob, to the farm for Thanksgiving dinner. Almost everything on our Thanksgiving dinner table had come from our farm: mashed potatoes, home-baked bread, boiled rutabagas, dill pickles, baked squash, pumpkin and apple pies, canned corn. Pa liked cranberries, so we always bought some fresh cranberries for Thanksgiving. Cranberries were about the only purchased item on the menu. I don't recall that we ever had turkey for Thanksgiving dinner. We tried to raise turkeys one year, but a fox got most of our small flock before they had grown to Thanksgiving size. Pa liked roast duck, so most years we had that. We raised Muscovy ducks, which somehow successfully avoided the ever-present predatory foxes and weasels. When we had no ducks, we relied on a plump chicken. Most years, Ma raised fifty or so White Rock roasters that she sold to various customers in town. We usually saved back a few of the plumpest birds for our Thanksgiving and Christmas dinners in the no-duck years.

The first snowfall usually arrived in November. I looked forward to the first measurable snow. We hauled our sleds from the space above the woodshed, found our skis, and looked forward to the fun side of snow and winter weather.

We began asking Pa as early as the first week in November, "When's it gonna snow, Pa?"

He'd smile and say, "Soon enough. Soon enough. Lots of work to do before it snows."

Each morning, we'd look at the sky as we walked to school, thinking about snowflakes and winter fun. One year, a day in mid-November, the first snowflakes began fluttering down as we walked to school. The first snowflakes of the year were things of beauty, especially for country kids who enjoyed winter. The snowflakes landed on our mackinaw coats and hand-knitted woolen mittens. They accumulated on the dead grass and fallen leaves along the road.

All morning, when we were supposed to be studying, we sneaked peeks out the schoolhouse windows at the falling snow. We hoped that by noon the snow would be deep enough so we could lay out the first track for fox and geese, a winter game we all enjoyed playing.

To play fox and geese, we packed the snow in a big circle, everyone in school walking one behind the other, following the leader, who was usually a seventh or eighth grader. At our school, the softball diamond lent itself to the construction of a great fox and geese track. Once the big circle was laid out, the leader walked across the circle, again with everyone following, to cut the circle in half and once more to divide the circle into quarters.

One player was designated the fox; all others were geese. The object of the game was for the fox to tag the geese until there were no geese left. The center of the circle was "safe," but only one player could be there at a time. A rule was for everyone to stay on the circle path or on one of the spokes. The game continued until the fox had tagged all the geese. The last person tagged became the fox.

By the end of November, ice fishing season started and continued into early March. On a cold Saturday morning, Pa would announce at the breakfast table that we ought to go ice fishing when the barn chores were done. Of course, my brothers and I enjoyed ice fishing for many reasons, not the least of which was avoiding odd jobs around the farm on cold winter Saturdays. Our old sleigh coupe—a building about four feet square with a tin roof, windows on three sides, and a sheet-metal woodstove—became our shelter for fishing. The little gray building had been used as a shelter on the horse-drawn bobsled, when Pa drove to town with a load of potatoes. Pa nailed a floor to the little building and, with a couple of two-by-four runners, we could drag it across the ice. Unfortunately, the ceiling was only about five feet from the floor, so you had to remember to not stand up fully or you'd crack your head on one of the wooden pieces that held the tin roof in place.

In those days, our favorite ice fishing location was Mt. Morris Lake, located seven or eight miles from our farm. Before using our new ice shanty, as structures on the lake were called, we had huddled onshore around a smoky little campfire trying to keep warm. Now, with our ice fishing shanty, we fished in style and stayed warm besides. Pa figured there was something wrong with cutting a hole in the new floor in our shanty, so we always fished outside and warmed up inside.

To catch northern pike, we used live minnows and little devices called tip-ups, which were made of a reel of fishing line and a wooden device that had a spring-loaded red flag that flew into the air when a fish grabbed the bait. To fish for bluegills, sunfish, crappies, and perch, we sat outside with a short fish pole called a jig-pole and watched a tiny bobber in the fish hole that was forever freezing over, especially on cold days.

We had lots of company on Mt. Morris Lake: the Nelson boys, who lived on Highway 22 south of town; our neighbors Jim and Dave Kolka; and often my uncle Wilbur Witt. Tex Keenlance often fished on the lake. I never knew his real first name. We always pronounced his last name as "Keen-eyes," which was way off the mark, but Tex didn't seem to mind. Tex was a few years older than me, tall and thin, and an excellent fisherman.

There were a bunch of other fishermen as well, usually all men and boys, but sometimes a woman would show up, and that would cause a serious problem when it was time to go to the bathroom. You always knew when there was a woman fishing because of the steady trail of men to the woods surrounding the lake.

We seldom let the weather keep us from ice fishing. A raging blizzard that closed the roads to travel was about the only impediment. Below-zero temperatures, or even sleet or moderate snow, did not keep us off the lake. On bad weather days, say when it was sleeting, the inside of our fish shanty was especially cozy. The sleet pounding on the tin roof, the warmth of the little stove, the smell of coffee mixed with wood smoke all contributed to a pleasant experience. On the most miserable winter days, we'd invite our friends into our shanty, until it was filled with the foul smell of wet wool and bad-smelling fishermen. But the stories made up for the smells. The stories made the hours fly by. On a good day, we might have only three or four bites on our tip-ups, so ice fishing left lots of time for storytelling and sometimes out-and-out lying, as some fisherman were inclined to stretch the truth now and again. Especially when they recalled fish they'd caught four or five years ago. A good rule of thumb when deciphering a fish story: for each passing year, fishermen add about two to three pounds to a fish's weight and six inches to its length. Can you imagine the monster fish caught ten years earlier? Unbelievable, but plausible to those of us kids who were listening to these exaggerated fish tales.

When the shanty was crammed full of fishermen on a bad weather day, it was a problem when a tip-up flag flew, meaning a northern pike had grabbed the bait and tripped the mechanism.

"Somebody's got a tip-up," a more serious fisherman, glancing out the window, would announce. Unfortunately, there was no way for six or eight overdressed fishermen to rush through our little fish shanty door at the same time. So in their excitement and hope that the fish biting might be on their line, they would push each other through the small door like BBs flying out the barrel of a Red Ryder air rifle. The ice fishing shanty would shake violently.

The Department of Natural Resources had a longstanding rule that by March all of the ice fishing shanties had to be removed from Wisconsin's lakes. It was good rule, for there were always fishermen who wouldn't get around to hauling their shanty home and it would float around in the lake after the ice went out, causing all kinds of problems.

One year, in February, the temperature rose above freezing for several days and it rained. All the lakes, including Mt. Morris Lake, were covered with three or four inches of water. We avoided fishing during the warm up, but then the temperature returned to below zero and the lake froze. Except now there was a lake on top of a lake—two layers of ice, one covering the real lake, and the other covering the meltwater and rainwater. Unfortunately, when we returned to our ice shanty, we discovered that it was frozen into this new top layer. Try as we might we couldn't chop it loose. Pa hoped for another warm spell before we had to remove the shanty from the lake, but none came. The deadline day was fast approaching.

To solve the problem, Pa brought along a saw one day and cut off the floor of the shanty at ice level. At least now we could remove the majority of the shanty and hope that no one would recall what the floor of our shanty looked like when it floated off in the spring.

Pa nailed a new floor on the shanty, but now the floor-to-ceiling height was about six inches shorter than in the old shanty. When we stood up, we had to stand hunched over, looking, I suppose, like our ancient relatives the Neanderthals. After a couple bashes against the ceiling, we all learned to accommodate to the new size.

Now, many years later, I think often of that little ice shanty, and the good times we had at Mt. Morris Lake, swapping stories, drinking coffee, eating sandwiches warmed on our little stove, and learning how to enjoy a winter day.

November, that transition time from fall to winter, is filled with memories. First snowflakes of the season. Playing fox and geese at the country school. Banking the house. Making wood. Thanksgiving dinner. Ice fishing.

November Thoughts

⌐ No work is so important as to prevent a day's fishing through the ice.

⌐ A cold wind blows from the northwest all day, tearing leaves from the aspens and oaks and sending them scurrying. As the sun sets, the wind dies and a great calm settles over the land. That which has been disturbed the entire day now has a chance to rest and recover from the relentless wind. I marvel at the contrast between the roar of the wind in the treetops and the silence when there is no wind at all. It's like life, with its periods of turmoil and agitation followed by quiet and calm.

⌐ Not far from my farm is a small spring-fed pond that is the beginning of Pine River. At its starting place, the Pine River is but a trickle of water that grows larger and more powerful as more springs add to it. The stream lazily moves along, gurgling over its gravelly bottom, sliding quietly around the bends where there are holes large enough for brook trout to hide. The river eventually pours into Lake Michigan and some days hence becomes a part of the Atlantic Ocean. In time, the water will return as it evaporates, clouds form, rain falls, and the little springs are replenished, repeating the cycle over and over again as the years pass.

～ On a cloudy, quiet late afternoon, I hike by the old white pine windbreak and listen to the sound of a woodpecker working on a dead tree. It's not just an ordinary woodpecker, but a seventeen-inch-tall pileated woodpecker, which has a long neck and a bright red crest on the top of its head. It is the largest woodpecker in our area and the loudest and most effective as it chisels two-inch-deep, six-inch-long rectangular holes in a dead white pine. Called a logcock by some, it chisels out wood chips often as large as an ax man's. It is a shy bird, usually heard and not seen. But today I see it, and I quietly watch it work.

～ We all live on the land and we are meddlers. We disturb, destroy, and transform the land, sometimes knowingly, often unknowingly. But the more we meddle, the more we are obliged to protect the land and its creatures. It is our obligation as human beings.

～ Country people face big and little problems, sometimes both in the same day.

～ I find a boulder deep in the woods to the north of the pond. It is as large as a compact car and has likely sat in this very place for ten thousand years, since the last great glacier receded, leaving behind these enormous stones and steep hills that defy the plow. The boulder is iron gray and covered with green lichens. I stand by it for a long time, realizing that not often do I have a chance to be near something so old and yet so massively sturdy, and so little touched by the years.

～ There is a difference between understanding and knowing. Understanding involves the mind; knowing requires the mind, plus the heart and the soul.

∼ Our lives are a series of little stories that add up to the big story of who we are, where we've been, what we believe, and what we value. Remembering and writing down the little stories is one way to communicate the big story of our lives.

∼ I think often about what a farmer has to understand: animals, crops, machinery, weather, marketing, financing, long-term planning, and more. He or she is a lawyer, a veterinarian, an accountant, a meteorologist, an agronomist, an engineer, a carpenter, a plumber, a market prognosticator, and a philosopher who is constantly asking why, how, and what is the meaning of it all. Consider all the wisdom that is lost when a farmer is forced off the land and moved to a minimum-wage job where that vast wisdom is neither wanted nor cared about.

∼ Near my farm are the remnants of an old, abandoned farmstead. All that remains is an old barn wall, the kind that was built a hundred years ago by stonemasons who took the stones from the fields and fashioned them into sturdy walls more than two feet thick. Besides holding up a barn, the walls were artistic creations of color and shape blending together like abstract art.

∼ Learn to putter. You putter when you dabble at a task and work at the edges. You putter alone, at your own pace, so that you have time to cogitate, meditate, or merely allow your mind to go blank. The result of puttering is contentment rather than completion.

∼ Sometimes when I watch a brilliant sunset, its pinks and reds and purples spreading across the sky, I think about what is most important in my life and what I cannot buy with money: sunsets, the love of a child, birdsong, wildflowers spreading across a hillside, the quiet of a dark night in the country, family, neighbors, and good friends. And I wonder why accumulating money is so important for so many people.

⟿ Everyone is of the land, related directly to it, for it is the land that provides food, materials for our buildings, fiber for our clothing, and a spiritual foundation for our souls. When we take the land for granted, or even worse ignore it, we are challenging humanity itself and its continued existence on this planet.

⟿ The afternoon is cloudy, and the wind starts, slowly at first, rustling the tops of the bare maples and then becoming a steady howl as tree limbs quake and shudder and the remaining dry leaves scatter. Soon the rain begins, horizontal and penetrating, hard rain, cold rain that by late afternoon turns to snow that drives visibility to zero. Winter is in the wings. Autumn is fighting a valiant battle and losing.

⟿ They come from the west, twelve of them, each with a black beard, and they assemble in the garden that I planted to winter rye earlier in the fall. Turkey gobblers. Some are giants with broad bronze backs and black beards that hang to the ground; others—jakes, they are called—are smaller, younger, with shorter beards. They pick at the green rye, eating lunch. Any doubt about the accuracy of the phrase "pecking order" is dispelled as the old gobblers peck at the jakes when they get in the way.

⟿ There are no shortcuts to important places.

⟿ As winter approaches, it is a time of waiting, a time beyond celebrating autumn and its vivid colors. Now all is brown and drab. The leaves have tumbled from trees that stand naked, and the wind moans as it moves through the bare branches. Winter is out there, waiting its turn. But until it arrives, we wait. The landscape waits.

~ Below-freezing temperatures overnight transform the northern ponds and lakes from water to ice—flat, shimmering, and glassy. With warming temperatures during the day and a stiff wind from the west, the ice will likely disappear before nightfall. But with a clear sky and dropping temperatures after sunset, the ice will reappear tomorrow. Winter returns a little at a time—forward, retreat, forward, retreat. But we all know that the inevitable will occur, that one day the ice will not melt and will remain until spring, each day becoming thicker and firmer. It is the cycle of nature and of life itself.

December

Christmas Program

In the 1940s, the Christmas season came early at our one-room country school. It started the Monday after we returned to school from a short Thanksgiving break. That very Monday afternoon, our teacher began talking about the upcoming Christmas program. "We'll put on an even better program than last year," she said. And we all knew she meant it, too, because in many rural school districts, the quality of the Christmas program was one important way that the community judged the worth of the teacher.

Theresa Piechowski, a tall, thin, black-haired young woman, was our teacher when I was in first grade. She had an impressive stack of little booklets in front of her, and she had been paging through them, looking for skits, recitations, musical numbers, and the like. Of course, I wasn't aware of it at the time, but she had at least two things on her mind. First, what would the community enjoy? That was tops on her list. Next was trying to match the various skits, songs, and recitations to the talents of the twenty or so students who made up the eight grades at our country school.

There were no music classes in those days. About the only music training we received was from *Let's Sing*, a radio program broadcast to all the country schools from the University of Wisconsin's WHA School of the Air. We did have some kids who sang well—an inherited gift, I would guess. Somehow, when the music genes were passed around, I must have been looking the other way, because I was told, sometimes gently and often not, that I couldn't carry a tune in a bushel basket. I early on realized that I wasn't going to be one of the lead singers in the Christmas program. The lead singers—alas, usually girls—got to sing "Away in a Manger" and other such important Christmas tunes, while the rest of us sort of mumbled in the background, trying to remember the words but keeping our lips moving no matter what. We knew that Miss Piechowski was watching each of us with an eagle eye. It would be a high-level offense to be caught not singing, even if you couldn't carry a tune.

Each of us, young and old alike, was required to give recitations. These were usually singsong poems about Christmas and its meaning, snow and its beauty, Santa Claus and his gifts, Christmas trees, elves, and the North Pole. I was a shy little guy, shorter and skinnier than my schoolmates and, at age five, had no desire to stand up in front of a crowd of neighbors and friends and make a fool of myself when I might forget a line in my recitation, or piece, as we referred to them. (I suspect the phrase "to say your piece" comes from speaking recitations at the country schools.)

That Monday afternoon following Thanksgiving, Miss Piechowski announced that each of us, from first graders to eighth graders, would be required to give recitations on the stage at the Christmas program. I held up my hand.

"Yes, Jerry," she said.

"I don't think I want to do a recitation," I said.

She had a surprised look on her face and a bit of a smile. Without any thought, any hesitation, not even a question of "why not?," she said simply and firmly, "Everyone will give a recitation at the Christmas program." And that was that. Case closed. One of my first challenges of authority squashed without even a hearing or at least a bit of discussion.

That night at home, I told my mother what had happened. My mother repeated the litany, "Everyone gives a recitation at the Christmas program." No sympathy or understanding at all. I sulked off to the woodshed to tote in wood for the wood-burning cookstove and the heater in our dining room, one of my everyday chores in those days.

Back at school the next day, Miss Piechowski took me aside during recess.

"Are you worried about giving a recitation at the Christmas program?"

"Yes, I am," I said. "Very worried. I'm not cut out for giving speeches." Frankly, I don't know how I got up the gumption to talk to her that way, but those were the words I said.

"You'll do just fine," she said.

"That's what Ma said, too. Ma said I'd do fine. How do you know I'll do fine? How does anybody know anything about what someone else can or can't do?"

I could see Miss Piechowski pondering that mouthful of words that sounded a little like how I had heard my Pa talk. Whenever I got in a tight place, I always tried to think of what Pa would say under similar circumstances.

"I'll share a trick that will make it easier for you," she said.

I couldn't imagine there were any tricks to speaking. As far as I could tell, people who gave speeches stood up in front of a bunch of people and talked, hoping to think of something to say. That's how it appeared to me anyway.

"Here's the trick," she said. She lowered her voice. "And you promise that you won't tell anybody what it is?"

"I won't tell a soul," I said, feeling a little smug that my teacher was letting me, a first grader, in on an important public-speaking secret.

"You stand on the stage, right near the front, and you take your hands out of your pockets and you put your shoulders back." She stood up and demonstrated how to do this. Somehow this part of the secret didn't impress me very much. She was tall; I was short. She was a girl; I was a boy. She wore a dress; I wore bib overalls. These differences were important, at least in my mind. But I didn't say anything.

"Once you've done that," she continued, "you use your outdoor voice." This came as a surprise to me, a monumental surprise, because all fall she had drummed into us, day after day, "Use your outdoor voices outdoors, your indoor voices indoors." Now she was saying the opposite. It was okay to use your outdoor voice inside, as long as you were standing on the stage and giving a recitation.

"But what if I forget my lines?" I asked. This was the part that terrified me. Standing on the stage with my hands at my sides, my shoulders back, and right in the middle of using my outdoor voice to say something profound, I would forget the words. Of course, part of the preparation for the program was to memorize everything, to "learn" all the lines in the skits, all the words for the songs, and every last word in the recitations.

"Here's what you do," she said. "Here's what you do so you don't forget your lines."

Now I was really paying attention because she was getting to the core of my concern.

"When you get up on that stage and look out in the schoolroom, you'll see your folks, your brothers, your fellow schoolmates, your neighbors, everybody in the community will be here."

"I know that, Miss Piechowski."

"I'll warn everyone to behave himself, but some of them won't. When you get up there somebody's going to make a face at you, maybe stick out his tongue, or cross his eyes, do something to make you forget your lines."

It was worse than I thought. Miss Piechowski obviously had a lot of experience with kids making other kids forget. All I needed was to see Jim Kolka crossing his eyes or my twin brothers, Darrel and Donald, sticking out their tongues at me. That would do it. My mind would go blank, and I would stand there on the stage with my hands out of my pockets and my shoulders back and my voice as silent as a frozen block of oak wood.

"Here's the trick," Miss Piechowski said.

Finally she was getting around to it. By this time she had just about convinced me that I should figure out a way to be sick on Christmas program night. The whole thing sounded like a disaster in the making.

"When you stand up there on the stage—," she began.

"Yes," I interrupted.

"Do you see the damper on the stove pipe back there?" she asked. She was pointing at the woodstove that heated our school. Why in the world was she changing the subject? What could the damper on the stove pipe—that little brown handle that controlled how much smoke went up the chimney—have to do with me forgetting my lines at the Christmas program?

"I see the damper," I said, going along with her digression.

"When you climb up on the stage to say your piece, look at the damper on the stove pipe."

"Look at the damper?" I said. "Why should I do that?"

"When you are looking at the damper, you won't see all the shenanigans that will likely go on. The damper will not stick out its tongue at you or cross its eyes."

I smiled. "Stare at the damper," I repeated, surprised at the simplicity of her secret weapon for avoiding stage fright.

"Works every time," she said, smiling.

Now, many years later, I fondly recall my first Christmas program at the Chain O' Lake school in central Wisconsin. The little schoolroom was packed with people from front to back. The Christmas program was the top social event for the community.

It was an opportunity for parents to see their kids on stage, for neighbors to see each other, and for everyone to have a good time. The school had no electricity, so for Christmas program night, Miss Piechowski lit two gasoline lamps that hung on either end of the schoolhouse, casting interesting shadows throughout.

The school building had no indoor plumbing either, so paths were well shoveled to the boys' outhouse on the south end of the school grounds and the girls' on the north end in preparation for the event. Miss Piechowski had a roaring fire in the big old rusty woodstove that stood in the back of the building. It provided ample heat—too much heat when the building was crammed full of people.

About two weeks before the Friday night of the program—always a Friday evening and the night Christmas vacation began—members of the school board nailed together a stage in the front of the schoolroom. The stage consisted of two-by-eight-inch wooden planks that were nailed to sawhorses. The stage stood about two feet off the floor. Board members strung a length of smooth wire from one side of the schoolroom to the other, in front of the stage. On the wire, Miss Piechowski fastened brown curtains that were stored in the piano bench. She used bed sheets to make side curtains for either side of the stage.

I recall how we had practiced each day, spending a little more time in preparations until the last week, when we spent every afternoon going over the songs, rehearsing the recitations, and doing the skits over and over again until we had them right, or at least right enough for Miss Piechowski's high but still reasonable standards. She knew she was dealing with a bunch of farm kids whose only connection to anything musical was listening to the Saturday night rendition of the WLS Barn Dance on their radios—most of them battery powered because electricity had not yet come to the farms in our community.

We got to the school a little early the night of the program. I wanted to be there in plenty of time so I could think through my recitation and make sure I had all the words forged in my mind. I also wanted to check one more time that I, short as I was, would be able to see the damper on the stove pipe when the room was filled with people. What good would my secret weapon be, my special strategy for speech giving, if I couldn't see the damper?

Soon the schoolroom was filled to capacity; it was standing room only, and people crowded the doors that led to the entryway. Miss Piechowski welcomed everyone—she was wearing a bright red dress that showed off her jet black hair. Then we all scampered on the stage and gave a rousing rendition of "Up on the Housetop," which received thunderous applause that filled the room. Next the upper-grade kids gave a series of boring recitations that the crowd seemed to like. The sixth, seventh, and eighth graders put on a little skit about Mrs. Santa Claus and her concern for her husband on Christmas night. Everybody clapped, even though a couple of the kids muffed their lines and had to have Miss Piechowski prompt them.

Then it was my turn to give my recitation. I was clearly the smallest kid in school—short, skinny—and my ears stuck out from my head more than they should have. But I was ready, and besides, I had a secret weapon.

I walked out on the stage, pushed back my shoulders, pulled my hands out of my overall pockets, and looked for the damper in back of the room. Where was the damper? A tall farmer, Bill Miller, was standing in front of the stove, and I couldn't see it. I wanted to yell out, "I can't see the damper," but I decided against it. If I had, Ma and Pa would think I had gone daft.

Just when I knew my mind was going blank, Bill turned and walked to the entryway for another block of wood for the stove. The damper was in clear sight, and I was on my way. I recited my entire piece to that damper, not forgetting a single word, and even remembering to emphasize certain words like Miss Piechowski had taught me.

I know I am prejudiced, but I believe I got an even bigger round of applause than when the entire school put on the nativity scene, where the baby Jesus, a naked doll in a sawbuck filled with straw, was watched over by Geraldine Hudziak wearing a sheet and Jim Steinke wearing a too-large bathrobe.

Now, so many years later, and hundreds, probably thousands, of speeches later, I still remember Miss Piechowski's encouragement and advice when facing an audience. Learning how to give a talk was one of the truly important lessons I learned from attending a country school. I wish I could thank this wonderful teacher now, for she knew how important it was to be able to stand up in front of a crowd and say your piece, even if you were a shy little farm kid more accustomed to talking to cows than to people.

December Thoughts

∽ Try asking the right question. The right question asked is often more than halfway to an answer.

∽ The morning sun has not yet crept above the white pines to the east. I watch a hen turkey under the bird feeder, only a few yards from the house. Warily, she picks at the leavings on the ground, always on the alert, watching, listening. She hears me in the cabin or catches my movement in the window, and she struts off, her long legs propelling her like a racehorse. But she will be back. Every creature enjoys a free lunch.

∽ As we destroy the natural world, a little at a time, we are destroying ourselves, a little at a time.

∽ I sit under a pine tree on a snowy day, when the only sound is that of snowflakes sifting through the pine branches. I can see only a few feet beyond where I am sitting because the snow is falling so heavily. I enjoy the isolation, the feeling that I am alone in the world.

∽ A good story, even if lacking in facts, can help us to see the truth.

～ Get acquainted with where you live. Learn the place's history. Study its geography. Become acquainted with its birds, its plants, its wild animals. But above all, listen for the stories of the people who live there. Stories tie us to a place, giving it meaning and depth and giving us a sense of permanence and belonging.

～ In December, I try to take time to assess the importance of what I have: family, health, freedom to create, friends.

～ Books do not scold when you blunder, laugh when you are ignorant, or hide when you seek them.

～ Watch the sun set on the shortest day of the year (December 21 or 22). Notice how far to the south it sets compared to the longest day of the year (June 21), when it sets away to the north. Take advantage of the long evening. Break out a bottle of wine you've been saving and share it with someone special. Light a candle. Listen to some good music.

～ I study the tracks—deer and rabbit mostly—that crisscross the open place in front of the cabin. The deer visit the garden, remembering the rye I planted in the fall and pawing through the several inches of snow to feast on a few mouthfuls of green. The rabbits search for seeds that the birds spill from the bird feeder. Hunger does not take a break, no matter what season.

～ After an early snow, slip on a pair of cross-country skis and slide into a black-and-white land where the evergreen trees add a green counterpoint. The only sound is that of the skis slipping over the snow.

～ Listen to the quiet on a night when the temperature hovers around zero, a cold moon hangs low on the horizon, and not a creature is stirring.

- Being consistent is a good thing, most of the time. But being inconsistent once in a while shakes up your friends and relatives who think they know you. Being a little mysterious can be kind of fun.

- Occasionally, you've got to keep going just to keep going, especially when you are a little older.

- On a December day, when there's a stiff breeze from the northwest challenging me at every step, I stop to watch a dead oak leaf skid across the surface of the snow, making a most interesting track. Like a sketch artist doing an abstract drawing with wiggles and curves, twists and turns, the leaf bounces along, driven by the wind.

- A young fellow got stuck in a blizzard. He walked to the nearest farmhouse seeking shelter. The farmer let him in but said his house was nearly filled with stranded travelers. "I do have room if you'll sleep on the couch with the red-haired schoolteacher," he said.

  "Sir," the young fellow said, "I am a gentleman."

  "So is the red-haired schoolteacher," replied the farmer.

- Appreciate the importance of waiting and the value of looking forward to something, as you enjoy what you are doing now. There are two approaches to happiness: gaining from the moment and looking joyfully forward to what is to come. As we work hard during the long days of summer, we wait for the slower days of autumn. As we enjoy winter, we look forward to spring.

- Who we are is where we've been, who our parents were, where we've lived, who our friends were and are. All of these influence what we see and how we see it, how we talk and what we say, how we think and what we think about, what we believe and what we value. We are our histories.

~ The greatest reward for a job well done is having done it.

~ Enjoy a bowl of oyster stew on Christmas Eve.

MA'S OYSTER STEW

1 pint fresh oysters
1 quart whole milk
1 tablespoon butter
1 teaspoon salt
¼ teaspoon pepper

In small pan, cook oysters over medium heat in the liquid they come in, stirring constantly until their edges curl.

Heat milk in larger pan on low heat. Add butter and stir until melted.

Add the oysters and liquid to the milk. Add spices and heat thoroughly.

Serves 4.

About the Author

A professor emeritus of agriculture at the University of Wisconsin, Jerry Apps grew up on a dairy farm in the 1940s. He has written more than forty fiction, nonfiction, and children's books. Recent books include *The Quiet Season: Remembering Country Winters*, *Whispers and Shadows: A Naturalist's Memoir*, *Never Curse the Rain: A Farm Boy's Reflections on Water*, and *Old Farm County Cookbook* (with his daughter, Susan Apps-Bodilly). Jerry's writing has won awards from the American Library Association, the Wisconsin Library Association, the Wisconsin Historical Society, and the Council for Wisconsin Writers, among others. He has created four documentaries about farm life and country living with Wisconsin Public Television. Jerry and his wife, Ruth, have three children, seven grandchildren, and two great-grandsons. They divide their time between their home in Madison and their farm, Roshara, near Wild Rose, Wisconsin.